If the Cat Fits ...

Stories of a vet's wife

CHRYSTAL SHARP

Illustrations by Jason Bronkhorst

PENGUIN BOOKS

PENGUIN BOOKS

Published by the Penguin Group
80 Strand, London WC2R 0RL, England
Penguin Putnam Inc, 375 Hudson Street, New York,
New York 10014, USA
Penguin Books Australia Ltd, Ringwood, Victoria, Australia
Penguin Books Canada Ltd, 10 Alcorn Avenue, Toronto, Ontario,
Canada M4V 3B2
Penguin Books (NZ) Ltd, Cnr Rosedale and Airborne Roads, Albany,
Auckland, New Zealand
Penguin Books India (P) Ltd, 11 Community Centre, Panchsheel Park,
New Delhi – 110 017, India
Penguin Books (South Africa) (Pty) Ltd, 24 Sturdee Avenue, Rosebank,
Johannesburg 2196, South Africa

Penguin Books (South Africa) (Pty) Ltd, Registered Offices:
Second Floor, 90 Rivonia Road, Sandton 2196, South Africa

First published by Penguin Books (South Africa) (Pty) Ltd 2001

ISBN 0141 00670 6

Typeset by CJH Design in 10.5 on 13.5 Palatino
Cover illustration: Jason Bronkhorst
Printed and bound by Interpak Books, KwaZulu-Natal

If The Cat Fits ...

 **S**outh **A**frican **V**eterinary **A**ssociation

Suid-**A**frikaanse **V**eterinêre **V**ereniging

All proceeds are committed to the **SOUTH AFRICAN COMMUNITY VETERINARY CLINICS** project, the South African Veterinary Association initiative to provide access to essential veterinary care for animals belonging to those unable to afford the services of a private practice.

Reg 01/02020/20 • Fund Raising No: 000-234 NPO

*For all the millions of animals out there
who have never experienced a loving home*

Contents

What is this thing in us
This Yearning
To soar
Like an injured eagle
One last time

Reaching out
We touch the elusive pulse
The Underlying Heartbeat
That is Life

A delicate filament
Oft-times dismissed
That we switch off
So lightly

Prologue

The gale-force wind gusted around us as we sped along the foaming waterline, bare feet padding soundlessly on the cool damp sand. Higher up on the beach the wind lifted the dry sand, hurling it on to sand dunes and bushes.

He touched my shoulder, his lips moving. The wind whisked the words from his lips and I shrugged helplessly. He gestured towards the sea, eyes speaking. I nodded, it was a magnificent sight.

Towering waves thundered in, one after another, breaking, colliding, sending sheets of white spray shooting into the air. Towards the horizon the sky was dark blue, almost navy, and grey-black storm clouds brooded overhead. The sea picked up the colour of the sky and in the east where the two met, a pale luminous glow heralded the approach of dawn.

The beach was deserted, not another soul in sight, as we and the three dogs raced on, glorying in the wild stormy weather. Our spirits thundered and crashed with the waves, then soared, swirling with the wind. Transcending the mundane, we became part of nature and the elements. Part of the underlying heartbeat.

Ahead, the bay veered inwards and for a few minutes we

faced the waves from the side, our eyes locked on dark blue, foam-crested tubes. Suddenly, before us, a massive black shape erupted from the water. It hung for a moment suspended against the sky before slowly toppling, crashing down, disappearing below the surface. Breathless, we stumbled to a halt. White spray spewed up, the only sign of its passage. My mind knee-jerked into action and I shouted, 'It must be a boat capsizing!'

We sprinted forward, rounding the curve of the bay, racing into the water up to our thighs. Facing the incoming waves, we scanned the surging surface for any sign of survivors. But there was nothing.

Then the waves seemed to part and once more it was there before us. A huge glistening hulk above the turbulent waters. This time we saw the tail flukes. And the callosities clinging to its sides. We were that close. Time and again, it exploded from the depths with the slow sure power of a colossus rising, slamming the water with the enormous flukes, then diving, cleaving the maelstrom. Side by side we stood, oblivious to everything except the pure exuberance of its movements. An exultation of life and freedom.

After a long while, I became aware of the icy water surging against my thighs. Shivering, teeth chattering, I touched his arm. 'We'll have to go back, Nic will be waking soon.'

Reluctantly, we turned towards the shore. The dogs were waiting on the sand, ears pricked, eyes unfathomable as they too sensed the primitive joy of the display.

With a last lingering look, we turned and jogged back towards home. As we went my mind ran free, reflecting on the twists and turns our lives had taken. Bringing us inexorably to this place.

Taking the Pulse

It had all started with Whippy really.

Even for a greyhound she was painfully thin. Her hip bones were sharp edges protruding from her body and on each hip was a large raw sore. Bedsores, I discovered later. A scar resembling a railway track ran down one thigh. I could count her ribs, and her light tan-coloured coat which should've been sleek and smooth was dull and moth-eaten. A pitiful sight, if it wasn't for the eyes. Those eyes! They were a warm velvety brown with flecks of gold and an expression of deep longing. It was her eyes I looked into when I glanced into her cage. When she saw me, her ears rose up like two question marks on her head.

We stood in the English sunlight, the thin dog and I.

A bee buzzed noisily past and she jerked, following it with her eyes, gazing at the sky in wonder, as if she'd never seen it before. Puzzled, I watched as she stood quite still, just gazing about her. Then, limping stiffly, she moved forward to sniff at the flowers growing against the wall, drinking in the smell of each blossom until her nose was powdered with pollen. It was a beautiful nose, like a large black cherry on the tip of her snout, and it whiffled from side to side as she smelled the flowers.

Suddenly, from behind us, a sharp voice sliced through the stillness.

'Mr Alberts will have your guts for garters.'

Jumping guiltily, we turned to meet the accusing glare of the senior receptionist.

'What do you mean?' I asked uncomfortably.

'That dog is not allowed to be taken out of the cage.'

'Why not?'

'Those were Mr Alberts' instructions.'

'But Mr Alberts hasn't been here in weeks.'

'Those were his instructions. Kindly take her back to her cubicle.'

Reluctantly, we entered the hospital section and as I opened the door to her cubicle, she limped slowly inside and then turned and gazed at me wistfully. I squatted down next to her and stroked her emaciated body. Her hair, dry and brittle, came away in my hand.

'Don't worry, I'll be back,' I whispered.

It was hard to walk away and I went and sat in the car to wait for Dave.

Dave and I had met just over a year before in South Africa, when he was doing a locum for a vet in my home town. The vet had been savaged by a security dog and Dave had been employed to run the practice until he recovered.

During his locum, my Siamese cat Blossom fell ill and I arranged to drop him off at the rooms on my way to work. Later that morning I telephoned to enquire about the diagnosis. After discussing the problem and the treatment there was a short silence and then Dave mumbled, 'What are you doing tonight?'

Taken aback, I stammered, 'Umm, nothing.'

'Would you care to accompany me to a dance?' he asked. 'OK.'

I had recently returned from Britain and the only formal dresses I possessed all had long sleeves and were totally unsuitable for a summer function. Unable to leave work myself, I telephoned my mother and asked her to find a dress for me.

'Chrystal, it's going to be difficult for me to choose a dress for you,' she protested.

'Mom, I've already agreed to go. I'm desperate, just bring something with no sleeves.'

'Why did you agree to go if you knew you had nothing to wear?'

'I'd already told him I wasn't doing anything tonight.'

'Well, why did you do that?'

'Because I thought he was going to invite me to watch an operation.'

I wasn't aware of it at the time, but Dave was less than enthusiastic about attending the dance. Unable to use them himself, the owner of the practice had pressurised Dave into making use of the dance tickets.

'They cost me a fortune,' he had said. 'It would be a waste if they weren't used.'

On our second date Dave took me to a cat show. He told me that he was planning to leave for Britain once the locum was over. My own ticket was booked for six months later and before he left we decided to link up in Britain and explore the country together. We corresponded while he was away and when I arrived in Britain, romance was in the chilly air. After a few months we became engaged and decided to marry when we returned to South Africa.

When we first met Whippy, Dave was doing a locum at a multi-man practice in a large city in East Anglia. The owner of the practice, Mr Alberts, had suffered a heart attack some weeks before and was expected to be off work for some time.

We were living in the countryside outside the city in a cottage that was situated in the grounds of a large property belonging to Penny and Russell, an English couple the same age as ourselves. They lived in the main house. Besides the cottage, there was a barn, an outhouse, a tennis court, an area of woodland and a stream. The cottage was a long narrow building with a bedroom at one end, a sitting-room with a fireplace in the middle and a small kitchen and bathroom at the other end. From the sitting-room we looked out on to an area of rough lawn bordered by forest with thick undergrowth.

We had been living there for several weeks when early one Sunday morning Dave suggested I accompany him to the practice since he was on weekend duty.

'There are two stray dogs you can walk while I'm consulting.'

At the hospital, he showed me the two strays in their cubicles and while he was busy with treatments, I took first one, then the other, around the block. It was one of those still, gentle days, the air filled with the sound of insects buzzing about their business.

The cages in the hospital were similar to shower cubicles, with a window set at eye-level in each door. As I closed the second stray in, I glanced through the window of the third cubicle. Two shining brown eyes gazed hopefully back at me.

'Hello, what's your name?' I said. 'You look as if you'd like to go for a walk too.' Dave was injecting a cat in one of the consulting rooms. 'Dave, what about the greyhound?' I asked. 'May I take her out?'

'Well, she's not on any treatment. Apparently she had a plating in her leg some time ago, which didn't take. Don't walk far with her, just let her enjoy the sunlight.'

When she realised that she was being taken out, her eyes lit up with delight. Rising awkwardly, she limped outside with me. So there we were, standing quietly in the sunlight, when we were informed what Mr Alberts would do with our intestines.

When Dave returned to the car, I was bursting with questions.

'Who does the greyhound belong to? Why does she look at the sky as if she's never seen it before?'

'I don't know, I've never seen anyone visiting her.'

I described the reaction of the senior receptionist and he shook his head in disbelief.

'There is no reason for her to be totally confined to the cage. Those bedsores could do with some sunlight. I'm sure there's been some misunderstanding. I'll make enquiries tomorrow.'

I needed to know. The expression in her eyes when I left her was haunting me. She was asking me for something. Throughout that night I tossed and turned in bed, remembering how her eyes had gazed into mine.

Dave spoke to the senior receptionist the next day and discovered that the dog was fourteen months old. At the age of six months she had been hit by a bus, badly fracturing one hind leg. Two platings had been performed on the damaged leg, but neither had taken, leaving a gap in the bone. She had spent eight months in the hospital cubicle –

more than half her life. Mr Alberts had been planning a third plating but the heart attack intervened. He had been away from the practice for several weeks when one of the other vets decided to put the dog down.

He felt it would be the humane thing to do and contacted her owners who gave their permission for the euthanasia. However, on hearing of this plan, the senior receptionist stepped in. She pointed out, very firmly, that Mr Alberts was extremely fond of the dog and that it would not do his heart any good to find that she had been euthanased.

The owners were under the impression that she was dead and the vet who had decided to euthanase her was reluctant to inform them that she was still alive. He did not want to cause them unnecessary grief, as he felt that ultimately the lack of healing in the leg would necessitate euthanasia.

'Dave, can't we take her to the cottage and build her up a bit?' I asked. 'She's in such a poor state for a third operation. She's pathetically thin and it must be so lonely in that cage, day after day.'

'That would depend on Alberts. Maybe I should visit him at home and see what he feels about it.'

'Please.'

I spent the next day in suspense, restlessly wondering if we would be allowed to take her. That evening when I heard the car pull in behind the cottage I hurried out. Dave smiled at me as the greyhound clambered awkwardly from the car.

And so Whippy came to live with us. A purely temporary arrangement.

Mr Alberts had agreed to her living with us until he was ready to operate. He asked Dave to call on the owners and explain the position. Dave had popped around to see them during his lunch-hour and they were happy with the arrangement, although naturally very surprised to hear that she was still alive.

Whippy was completely overwhelmed with happiness at being with us. As we took her into the cottage, her whole body quivered with delight, her tail making huge circles in the air, her eyes radiant with joy, as if she couldn't believe she was finally out of the cubicle. Eight months is a long time.

Penny had seen Dave arrive and came over to meet Whippy. Taking one look at her, she exclaimed, 'Dear heaven, what has happened to this dog? She's so *thin*! She looks as if she escaped from a concentration camp.'

Whippy loved Penny. In fact, we were to discover that she loved all people and all animals. Her heart was huge and there was room in it for everybody and everything.

Penny left, but returned five minutes later with a large bowl of eggs.

'They're for Whippy,' she said.

We mixed the eggs with dog pellets and Whippy polished them off in a matter of seconds, eagerly looking around for more. In the days that followed, she seemed to be perpetually hungry. Three bowls of food a day were not enough.

One morning, in desperation, I filled a bucket with food: eggs, pellets, bread and milk.

'OK, now eat that and tell me you're still hungry,' I smiled complacently.

Glancing at me happily, she waded in. When I returned a few minutes later, I gazed at the scene before me in disbelief. The bucket was empty and Whippy had her snout in a tin of strawberry jam which she'd stolen from the dresser.

Life with her was not without its problems. Because she had been confined to a cage for so long, she was no longer house-trained. The cottage had fitted carpets with a sponge underfelt and when I entered the sitting-room in the mornings, I would cringe at the sight of more than one stool and several wet patches.

'Oh no,' I'd groan. The amount of food she was consuming did not help matters. I spent many long hours trying to dry the carpet with my hairdryer. A hopeless task really. Dave brought newspapers home and at night we laid them on the target areas. After a while the situation improved as Whippy realised that doing her business in the house was displeasing to us. It was very difficult to put this across. The hurt look in her eyes if we scolded her left us feeling guilty. Both physically and emotionally, she was very vulnerable.

It didn't take me long to discover that Whippy hated to be left alone. The day after her arrival I closed her in the cottage and set off for the village shop, intending to buy cigarettes and bread. It was an hour's walk each way and too far for her with her damaged leg. The piercing wails that emerged before I had even left the property forced me to abandon the plan rather hastily. Now that she had found us, Whippy did not intend to lose us.

I phoned Dave at the practice and asked him to buy bread and cigarettes on his way home.

'Aren't you going to the village today?' he asked, surprised.

'No, I can't.'

'Why not?'

'Whippy doesn't like being left alone.'

'Chrystal, don't be silly, she'll get used to it.'

'I don't think so.'

Replacing the receiver, I stared glumly at my empty cigarette packet. It was going to be a long day.

When he entered the cottage that evening, Dave paused, sniffing the air. 'My God, what is that foul smell?'

'Rosehip cigarettes,' I muttered, diving for the shopping

bag in his hand.

'Are you trying to give up again?'

'No.'

A few days later, Penny came to me with a small request.

'Russell and I are going away for two weeks. Would you feed the hens and rooster for me?'

'Of course, it'll be a pleasure.'

She showed me where the feed was stored in the barn and asked me to scatter it in the courtyard every morning. The rooster and hens ranged freely over the property, but usually gathered in the courtyard to be fed.

On the first morning of their absence, I said to Whippy, 'Now be a good girl and stay here, while I go and feed those hens.'

She wagged her tail happily as I closed the door, but as I rounded the side of the cottage, frantic howls erupted from inside.

'*HOOOOOO . . . HOOOOOO.*'

Sighing heavily, I trudged back.

'Whippy, don't be difficult. It'll only take a few minutes.'

She licked me lovingly. Closing the door, I strolled towards the barn. Within seconds, frenzied barking and howling followed me, echoing through the once peaceful neighbourhood. Pausing only to grab the bucket of feed, I rushed back to the cottage. As I opened the door, the ear-splitting howl stopped abruptly as she jumped up, delighted to welcome me back after all this time.

'You're being very silly,' I said severely, wagging my finger at her. 'If the hens don't eat, you won't get any eggs.' Penny had been extremely generous in her supply of eggs for Whippy.

She nodded understandingly. I patted her on the head and left, closing the door behind me yet again. Leaning against the door, I waited.

It took a split second for her to build up enough steam.

'*HOOOOO . . . HOOOOO.*'

OK, I thought, this is not going to work. I'll have the neighbours around in droves to discover the source of the noise and to complain. Especially to complain. Sound travelled through the countryside, especially sounds of a high-pitched nature. I found a length of thin rope in the barn. Whippy ecstatically assumed she was being taken for a walk but I tied her to a fence-post at the corner of the cottage. Even if I wasn't in full view all the time, I could still shout to her.

Sweating and harassed, I hurried towards the courtyard where the hens and rooster were foraging. Agonised moans followed me.

'It's all right, Whippy. I'm coming!' I yelled.

'*HOOOOO . . . HOOOOOO.*'

As I approached, the rooster lifted his head, fixing me with a gimlet eye. He looked suspicious and one could hardly blame him, I thought, with me shouting like a lunatic and the air resounding with Whippy's howls. As the hens clucked happily and moved towards me, the rooster started pawing the ground with his feet. Then, as I lifted my hand to scatter the feed, he spread his wings and charged.

I turned and ran, dropping the bucket and scattering feed as I went. Fast, but not fast enough. He launched himself at me, embedding his talons in my calves.

Now my screams joined Whippy's howls. 'Aaaaah . . . AAARGH!' Fortunately, he loosened his hold within seconds and, swaggering with victory, turned back to the 'girls', who

were now feeding contentedly on the spilt food.

As I tottered back to the cottage Whippy greeted me with squeals of joy. As if I'd been away for days. Collapsing into a chair and examining my bleeding calves, I viewed the coming two weeks with a jaundiced eye.

In the two long weeks that followed, I matched my cunning against that of the rooster, sneaking around outbuildings and peering furtively around corners in an attempt to throw the feed before he spotted me. Once, I was trapped for an hour in a willow tree while he strutted aggressively below. The thing to remember about willow trees is that they bend. Another time, running wildly into the barn and just managing to shut the door in his face, I provided the visual effects while Whippy provided the sound.

'*HOOOOOO . . . HOOOOOOOO.*'

As the days slipped by, Whippy settled comfortably into our lives and our hearts. With her thin coat and ravaged body, she was severely affected by the cold and we made a bed for her on the couch, spreading a duck-down sleeping-bag over the cushions. She needed a soft surface because her bones were very prominent. We had noticed that hard surfaces caused her discomfort.

At bedtime, ensconced on her soft bed and covered by a thick blanket, she would close her eyes gently.

'*Now I lay me down to sleep,*' her face said.

Not ten minutes later, in the dark, an ice-cold nose would insert itself cautiously under the duvet at my feet. Creeping carefully upwards, it would be followed by a head, a few legs, a body and finally a tail. When this was achieved without eliciting any reaction from me, with a grunt and a sigh she would sink immediately into a deep untroubled sleep. I would lie still, pretending to be asleep, reluctant to cause her embarrassment.

When I woke in the morning I would gaze into Whippy's face on the pillow next to mine, lips blowing in and out as she breathed.

This desire to be close to us physically was more than a quest for warmth and a soft bed. Instinctively we knew that when she was close to us she felt safe and secure, the nightmare of a pain-filled past kept at bay. The physical scars written on her body were a reflection of emotional scars written on her mind.

Up in the Air

Three weeks after Whippy came to live with us, my friend Claire phoned from Dorset. She was coming to visit.

'We can explore the countryside in your Combi.'

'Umm . . . there is a slight problem. I didn't apply for an international driver's licence before leaving South Africa.'

'Well, why would anyone ask to see your licence?'

That was true. After all, I was a competent driver with a valid South African licence. I had simply omitted to apply for an international one before leaving home. Now that I was in England, I could not apply without the rigmarole of taking a driving test.

Claire said she would be travelling up by train from Dorset and we arranged to meet at Colchester station on a Monday at twelve noon. At twelve noon, Whippy and I were hopelessly lost somewhere in the middle of Colchester. Arriving at the station one hour late in a state of nervous tension, I hurried on to the platform with Whippy at my side. Claire was sprawled calmly on a bench, reading a book.

'Sorry we're late, we got lost,' I explained breathlessly.

'Not to worry,' she smiled.

14

Claire was British. We had met five years before, when we both worked at a hotel-cum-sailing school on the west coast of Scotland.

Claire lived on a different plane. She was unfazed by ordinary, everyday crises and I often wondered if she was even aware of them. For some reason, this ability of hers to sail serenely through life tended to create more stress in the people around her. Events which occurred on the day we first met illustrate this aspect of her personality perfectly.

The hotel had been without a cook for four weeks. It was a crisis situation. The previous cook had departed prematurely in a state of emotional distress after being chased around the kitchen by an indigenous species of black-faced sheep called Fred. After urgent advertising and many phone calls, Claire was appointed and collected from the station in Fort William on the specified day. The rest of the staff heaved a sigh of relief. Originally employed as general assistants, waiters, waitresses and cleaners, the strain of producing Scottish *haute cuisine* twice daily was taking its toll. My own talents were limited to arranging oatcakes artistically on a plate. The others were not much better.

The manager, Joan, was a pleasant person under normal circumstances. However, while bearing the brunt of preparing menus and meals to cordon bleu standard, she underwent a transformation. She became a shrieking harridan whom the rest of the staff tried their utmost to avoid. Which made her job even more difficult. By the time Claire arrived, the situation had become extremely volatile.

On the evening of Claire's first day, approximately an hour before dinner was due to be served, we were all assembled in the kitchen to await instructions from the new cook. Who wasn't there. Joan strode into the kitchen and stopped abruptly. 'Where is Claire?' she asked.

15

We shook our heads, no one knew. We looked on, poker-faced, as Joan contemplated an immediate nervous break-down, only to dismiss the idea. With admirable self-control, she commanded: 'You . . . peel the vegetables . . . You . . . prepare the starters.'

An hour later I saw Claire cycle past the kitchen windows.

'Oh look, there's Claire now,' I said to Joan.

Joan stormed out. 'Where have you been?' she demanded hysterically.

'Exploring the hills,' replied Claire, rolling her eyes vaguely.

'But . . . you were supposed to be preparing the dinner!'

'Oh . . . sorry. I'll just go and change.' She smiled gently at Joan.

As I got to know Claire in the days that followed, I dis-covered a brain like a razor blade lurking beneath the facial expression of a village idiot, and a tendency to utter 'Oh aarr' at intervals.

As she pored over a map of the area after supper, Claire pointed to Snape Maltings. 'There's a beautiful old mill here. I'd like you to see it.'

When I examined the route I realised that we would have to pass through the centre of Ipswich.

'Ipswich is a big city,' I said. 'We'll have to leave very early or wait until mid-morning to avoid the rush hour.'

I hadn't driven the Combi very often and my confidence was a bit lacking.

'Let's leave early then,' she said. 'If we can get away by quarter to seven, it should be fine.'

It should've been fine, except for one thing. I had forgotten about Joan's desperate attempts to wake Claire in the mornings.

'Claire, Claire, wake up, the guests are already seated!' she would shout, flinging stones at Claire's caravan. The stones gradually increased in size, until huge boulders were smashing against the metal exterior. Claire was not an early riser.

The next morning, after a leisurely breakfast, she pronounced herself ready. We left the cottage just before eight and when we entered Ipswich we immediately encountered heavy traffic. We crawled through the city, both myself and the Combi threatening to overheat. It took over an hour to reach the outskirts. At last we were in the countryside and I began to relax. I was driving happily along when I rounded a corner to find a British Army roadblock. Breaking out in a cold sweat, I joined the queue of cars.

'Why would anyone ask to see my licence?' I remarked bitterly.

'There is quite a lot of army activity in these parts,' Claire informed me. 'They often have roadblocks for training purposes, you know.'

Glaring at her, I managed not to comment. By the grace of God, they did not ask to see my licence and I pulled off jerkily through the barrier. A few miles further on, as I was beginning to recover my calm, Claire exclaimed, 'Oh look, we've driven past the Old Mill. Chrystal, stop quickly, turn back.'

'Hold on, we'll have to find a place where the road widens so that I can make a U-turn.' Narrow English country roads do not lend themselves to U-turns by Combis.

Eventually we came upon a small dirt track leading off the road. It was bordered by long grass on either side. I pulled off the road on to the track and began reversing into the grass in order to turn. As I did so, there was a sudden *thump*. The Combi stopped moving and tipped backwards. Claire and I stared at each other. Switching off the ignition, I eased the driver's door open. The whole vehicle rocked alarmingly.

'Don't move,' I said carefully to Claire. 'Just stay sitting and try to keep Whippy in the front seat with you.'

Whippy was already agitated at the idea of my leaving the vehicle and whined worriedly as I slid cautiously from the seat on to the ground. As I turned towards the back of the vehicle, the problem became obvious. The rear wheels of the Combi were suspended in mid-air above a deep ditch which had been concealed by the long grass.

'Now what do we do?' I muttered grimly.

'Can you see anything?' Claire called out.

'Yes, the back wheels are hanging over a ditch.'

'Shall I get out and help push?'

'No, stay put. I think it might tip backwards if you get out.'

My mind pictured the Combi tilting like an earthbound Titanic, as it submerged slowly beneath the grass. This is all Claire's fault, I thought moodily, kicking at a clump of grass.

Sighing heavily, I climbed down into the ditch and stared hopelessly at the two rear wheels suspended above my head. As I was standing there, two young women on bicycles approached.

'You have trouble?' they called out in broken English. They were French. I explained the situation and soon all three of us were in the ditch trying to shift the vehicle.

'Cannot *she* help?' one gestured towards Claire, who was relaxing in the front seat with a book. I replied that she was anchoring the vehicle and Whippy.

Except that she was not doing such a good job with

Whippy. Frantic at being separated from me, Whippy kept scrambling to the back of the Combi causing it to rock dangerously.

'*Hoooo . . . Hooooo.*'

'Claire, please keep Whippy in the front.'

'I'm trying.'

'Try harder.'

As we attempted to lift and push, brambles growing in the ditch tore at our legs and arms and my hair was a tangle of grass seeds. Every few minutes when we paused for a brief rest, I climbed up the embankment and stared nervously down the road. My greatest fear was the possible arrival of the British Army. Under circumstances such as these they would surely demand to see my licence.

As I stood staring down the road during one of these breaks, a white station wagon came by and stopped.

'Is there a problem, love?' the driver asked.

Once again I explained, and he, his wife and their three children joined us. Now there were eight of us in the ditch.

The man suggested that Claire start the engine and accelerate while we pushed. As we were heaving, sweating and breathing in exhaust fumes, the tune of *On the first day of Christmas* tinkled through my head. *Two French girls, three British kids . . . and a Combi in a big ditch*. The partridge in the pear tree was superfluous. Now that Claire was behind the wheel she could not even attempt to control Whippy, who was peering anxiously from the back window and adding her weight to the problem.

As we took another break, lolling exhaustedly against the Combi, a green van screeched to a halt. A man wearing a flat cap stuck his head out the window and shouted, 'What's up, mate?'

He joined us in the ditch and stared silently at the

suspended rear wheels. There were now nine of us in the ditch. It was a very large ditch.

'You need a rope, mate, that's what you need. Might have one in the van.'

I accompanied him to the van. As he opened the back door, I recoiled at the sight of a pile of dead rats, a ferret and what looked suspiciously like a fox. Then I noticed the sign on the side of the van: MR EXTERMINATOR. Digging around amongst the corpses, he produced a thick rope with a triumphant 'Aha!'

We tied it to the back of the van and to the front bumper of the Combi. While he climbed in behind the wheel of the van, we got back into the ditch. As he and Claire revved viciously, the rest of us pushed. Within seconds the two rear wheels spun back on to solid ground, mud and grass spewing into our faces.

A cheer went up from the crowd. I thanked everybody and then watched The Exterminator and the British family, looking somewhat the worse for wear, pull off in their vehicles. The French girls pedalled off shakily down the lane. I hoped they didn't have far to go.

As I climbed into the Combi, I glanced at myself in the rear-view mirror and realised that I looked a mess. Sweating and grimy, sprinkled with bleeding bramble scratches and mud, and tufts of grass appeared to be growing from my head.

Claire, I noticed, was still beautifully groomed. As we pulled off in the direction in which we had been travelling, she said, 'But Chrystal, what about Snape Maltings?'

The air was filled with the sound of heavy breathing as I fought the battle to control myself. And lost. Like a computer, my mind scanned its banks for an expletive that would express my feelings aptly. I found one, a word that I had never used in my life before, but under the circumstances . . .

'Claire,' I enunciated coldly.

'Yes?'

'Fuck Snape Maltings.'

And we drove on in silence through the glorious English countryside.

But later that day on our return trip, we *did* stop at Snape Maltings. It was well worth a visit. A few weeks later, Claire sent me a photograph of myself and Whippy standing in front of the Old Mill. On the back she had written, 'Remember this day?'

How could I ever forget?

That evening, feeling rather drained, I prepared supper for the three of us. Claire, I noticed with misgiving, had spread her map over the sitting-room carpet and was crouched over it, totally absorbed.

'What are you doing?' I asked casually.

'I'm deciding where we should go tomorrow.'

'We could stay here and swim in the river. It would be nice and restful.'

'I'm quite rested, thank you, and, besides, there are so many places I'd like to show you.'

'*Abandon hope all ye who leave here,*' was my immediate thought.

Hacking viciously at the carrots I heard her telling Dave about a famous Essex witch who had been burnt at the stake.

'The village where she lived is not too far from here.'

'Oh really?'

'Yes and they've converted her cottage into a museum. I'd like to show Chrystal the museum tomorrow.'

'Claire, remember we can't visit places where dogs aren't allowed,' I shouted from the kitchen.

'Of course dogs are allowed. Why wouldn't they allow dogs? This is England. We love our dogs.'

'NO DOGS ALLOWED' said the sign affixed firmly to the door of the museum.

We contemplated it in silence.

'I'll wait in the Combi with Whippy,' I offered.

'No, don't be silly, there won't be anyone here to enforce it. I particularly want you to see the house.'

With these words Claire pushed the door open and sailed inside. As Whippy and I followed, a man rose from a chair just inside the door. Catching sight of Whippy, a flicker of annoyance crossed his face.

'Madam,' he said heavily, addressing me, 'there is a sign outside which clearly states that dogs are not allowed. Can you not read?'

Red-faced with embarrassment I turned to leave and Claire followed.

'There won't be anyone here to enforce it,' I said in a sarcastic tone.

'I think he's being unreasonable,' Claire stated loftily.

'And he thinks we're being illiterate.'

'Never mind about him. We can leave Whippy in the Combi, we won't be away long.'

'Claire, Whippy doesn't like being left.'

'Chrystal, look, the Combi is parked right below the windows. We'll be able to see her from inside.'

'That's not the point. She's going to make a lot of noise.'

'I'm sure she won't,' Claire smiled at Whippy who gazed back adoringly.

Rolling my eyes heavenwards, I unlocked the sliding door and clambered in to open a few windows.

'Just wait here, we won't be long,' I told Whippy. Her eyes clouded over with worry as I shut the Combi door, leaving her inside.

As we entered the museum we mingled with a group of Japanese tourists slung with cameras and binoculars. Halfway up the narrow staircase – with Japanese before us and Japanese behind – we heard the first howl.

'*Hoooo*,' came the muted sound.

'You see, it's barely audible,' said Claire reassuringly.

It may have been barely audible but the couple ahead of us heard it. The woman lifted her head as if sniffing the air while her partner looked around uneasily.

'She's just starting,' I whispered to Claire.

'Pardon?'

'It's going to get louder.'

And it did.

'*HOOOOOO*,' came the next howl as we entered the witch's bedroom.

'Chrystal, have a look at this,' Claire paused before a photograph hanging on the wall. Ignoring her, I watched the group. They had all heard the second howl and were huddled together, glancing apprehensively over their shoulders.

'*HOOOOO . . . HOOOOO . . . HOOOOOO.*'

This third howl, one of Whippy's best, broke the nerve of the group. As one, they turned towards the staircase. There was some confusion as they jostled for position, cameras and binoculars colliding violently. It was a very narrow staircase.

Whippy's howls were coming fast and furiously and finally, when the staircase was clear, I hurried down. The man at the door gave me a nasty look. I pretended not to notice.

Outside in the street a small crowd had gathered around the Combi. Whippy was playing to an audience. As I inserted the key into the lock, a buxom woman with flaming red hair called out, 'Shouldn't that dog see a veterinarian? She's in a terrible state.'

'She sees a veterinarian every day,' I hissed. 'And she looked much worse when we got her.'

Whippy greeted me with squeaks of delight, overjoyed to see me again after all the years we'd been apart.

The Lost Isles

As the weeks went by spring departed, leaving summer in its stead. Blissfully sunny days unwound into long mellow evenings.

When Dave came home from the practice we would stroll through the countryside, gradually increasing the distance as Whippy's condition improved. Reacting to the countryside as if it was brand new, straight from the box, she delighted in each new discovery. Her nose couldn't take in enough smells. Green fields with hedgerows and thickets in full bloom, banks of wildflowers and ripe juicy blackberries. One evening we came upon an old church surrounded by ancient oaks, where mouldering graves lay peacefully in the soft golden light.

'If she keeps this up, she's going to need a new one,' I murmured, pausing to watch Whippy.

'A new leg?' asked Dave.

'No, a new nose.'

We had discovered a slow meandering river only ten minutes' walk from the cottage and as the weather grew warmer, the desire to swim became irresistible. One evening, having donned swimming costumes under our clothes, we undressed under the trees at the riverside and slipped into the cool brown water. Whippy, left on the bank, was beside herself.

'*HOOOOO . . . HOOOOOO*,' she howled and the next instant she had flung herself into the water after us. As we floated lazily to and fro, Whippy swam round and round us. Once she had overcome the strangeness of being in water, she relaxed. If it was possible for a tail to wag under water, then Whippy's was wagging. All the time.

The evening swim became a regular event. Afterwards we strolled slowly back to the cottage, tingling and refreshed. Sometimes we collected pieces of dry wood lying in the field and we'd make a fire in a clearing outside the cottage and cook our dinner on it. For Whippy, it was heaven. She would curl up contentedly next to the fire, staring into the glowing coals and thinking deep thoughts.

'Mike and Lent phoned me this morning,' Dave said when he arrived home one evening.

'Oh?'

'There's a bank holiday coming up and they suggested that we all go to Wales for a long weekend.'

'What about Whippy?'

'She can come too. We'll sleep overnight at camping sites, it shouldn't be a problem.'

Mike and Lent, a South African couple whom Dave had known for years, drove up from London a few days later. Mike was completing a law degree at London University and Lent was working as a haematology technician. They decided to leave their car at the cottage and travel with us and had brought a small tent to sleep in. Dave, Whippy and I would sleep in the Combi.

We set off early on the Friday morning, Mike and Lent on

the rear bench seat and Whippy perched between Dave and me in the front. The miles sped by and after a few hours we turned off the motorway on to a single lane road. There was a stream of cars ahead of us. We slowed down, almost coming to a halt as we drew up behind the last vehicle.

'There appears to be a problem ahead,' Dave muttered.

'Maybe there's been an accident,' Lent suggested, as we crawled along at snail's pace. There was no possibility of overtaking, the vehicles were bumper to bumper as far as the eye could see.

'What on earth is going on?' Dave exclaimed in exasperation as the temperature gauge on the Combi edged into the red. 'We'll have to stop soon and allow the engine to cool.'

Thirty minutes later we spotted a service station. The parking area was crammed with cars and people were milling around.

'We might as well fill up with petrol,' Dave said, pulling in.

While he chatted to the petrol attendant, we drifted over to the restrooms. When we returned, Dave turned to us with a wry look. 'It's not an accident.'

'What is it then?'

'We're queuing for Wales.'

Having never queued for a country before, we were astounded. I looked at the line of cars stretching into the distance and hoped that it wouldn't be full when we got there. 'WALES FULL – TRY SCOTLAND.'

An hour later the traffic began to thin as vehicles peeled off for different destinations and at last we were able to travel at a reasonable pace. We planned to spend the weekend in the forested hills at the foot of the Black Mountains and as Dave drove, Lent scanned the map. Huge trees formed a canopy overhead and at intervals there were signs warning that open fires were not permitted.

'According to the map, the next village is the last before we reach the camping site,' Lent said. 'I think we should stop there and buy any supplies we need for tonight.'

At the word 'supplies' Whippy's eyes lit up.

'You needn't worry, your food is packed,' I told her. Looking crestfallen, she hung her head. 'Well, all right, maybe a liver sausage,' I relented and she perked up.

We found a small general dealer's shop in the main street of the village. Stretching our stiff limbs we climbed down from the Combi. As we entered the shop, I drifted over to the newspaper stand while the others discussed the supper menu.

'You poor thing! Whatever has happened to you?'

I swung round to see Whippy standing before the shop-keeper, gazing up at the elderly lady with glowing eyes.

'You're so *thin*! Here, have a sausage.' Whippy wolfed down the sausage as if she hadn't eaten for days. The old lady stared at me accusingly. 'Why is this dog so thin?' she demanded in a thick Welsh accent. 'And what are these terrible sores on her body?'

'They're bedsores,' I replied as Whippy bit into another sausage, smacking her lips as it disappeared down her throat.

'Bedsores?'

'Yes, she's recovering from an operation.'

'Ah, the poor wee thing!' she exclaimed. Whippy rolled her eyes pathetically and yet another sausage was produced from behind the counter.

'I'll have this newspaper and a liver sausage for the dog.'

'Just the one liver sausage?'

'Yes, please.'

'My dear, one liver sausage is hardly enough for this dog.

She needs building up.'

'We *are* building her up.' I glared at the woman, picturing the mounds of food Whippy consumed on a daily basis. 'We have her dogfood in the Combi.'

'I always say,' the old lady continued, 'that if you keep an animal, you must be prepared to look after it.'

'We do look after her.'

'After all, they can't speak for themselves, can they?'

Looking at Whippy, I wasn't too sure of this. She appeared to be coping very well without words.

'May I pay for the newspaper and sausage, please?'

The others were still deep in discussion amongst the foodshelves and I decided to wait in the Combi.

'There is such a thing as laying it on too thick,' I remarked caustically as we left the shop. Whippy avoided my eyes, her tongue flicking out to sweep up the last crumb of sausage adhering to her nose.

'And what's more, if you get carsick, we'll know the reason why.'

She burped gently.

Shortly after our weekend in Wales, Penny came to me with the news that they were going away again, to Brussels, this time only for a week.

'Chrystal, will you feed the chickens for me?'

'Oh no!' I stared at her in dismay.

'You can scatter the feed at night, when the rooster's asleep.'

'All right then.'

The rooster and I were still not sitting before the same henhouse. There were regular skirmishes and now Whippy was terrified of him too. When confrontations took place I would yell, 'Run, Whippy, run!'

It was every man for himself and streaking past me in pursuit of cover, she beat me every time, despite her gammy leg.

Apart from feeding the chickens, Penny had asked if I would water the plants in the hothouse twice a day.

On the first afternoon of their absence we were on our way to the hothouse when Whippy and I came upon a man crouched over a molehill near the barn. He had a canister fitted to a pump which he was inserting into the molehill.

'What are you doing?' I asked pleasantly. Startled, he turned towards me and I recognised him as a neighbour of Penny and Russell's. We had met before.

'Ooops . . . you gave me quite a turn,' he said. 'I'm pumping poison into the molehills. The moles are wreaking havoc with the lawn.'

'I don't think Penny would like that,' I said firmly.

'Russell asked me to do it while they were away,' he explained uneasily.

'Penny loves the moles, she told me so,' I said even more firmly.

He muttered something under his breath.

'I think you should wait and ask Penny's permission when she returns.'

I stood my ground and when he realised that I had no intention of leaving him to poison even one mole, he packed up and left, muttering to himself.

On Penny's return I told her about this incident. 'Russell wouldn't do something like that, would he?'

'I don't know, but I'll find out.'

Furiously, she confronted Russell.

'I deny all knowledge of it,' Russell exclaimed vehemently.

'I know you love moles and I wouldn't *dream* of having them poisoned behind your back.'

We decided that the neighbour had acted on his own initiative.

As the weeks went by, there was a visible improvement in Whippy's walking. The limp became less pronounced and she showed a tendency to run in open spaces. The swimming seemed to be working wonders.

'I'm going to take Whippy in for an X-ray,' Dave said one morning, and took her off to the practice with him for the day. That evening when they returned Dave was smiling broadly. He handed me the X-ray. It showed a bridging callus formation of bone, where before there had been a complete non-union. She would not be needing the third operation.

Suddenly September was upon us. The locum was coming to an end as Mr Alberts, now almost fully recovered, would be returning to his practice soon.

Originally we had planned to spend some time in the Greek Islands before returning to South Africa. We had estimated that by the end of the locum we would have saved enough money for two weeks on the islands.

But what about Whippy?

We discussed it over and over again, sometimes with Whippy looking anxiously from me to Dave, sensing that something was wrong.

'We can't leave her, she loves us so much.'

'I know, but she doesn't belong to us.'

'Maybe we should ask her owners.'

'Ask them what?'

'If we can have her.'

'Then what?'

'Then we'll take her home. Dave, can you imagine how she'd enjoy the beaches?'

'Yes. But what if they say no?'

This usually ended the discussion for a few days, as the implications of loving a dog who did not belong to us sank in.

Eventually, Dave plucked up the courage to go and see her owners who lived in a house with a small garden on a busy bus route. They were thrilled to see Whippy, but they were concerned that she was the wrong breed of dog for their situation. If she ventured into the road she would be run over again. They said that we could keep Whippy. Dave hugged them and Whippy hugged them even harder.

'What about the Greek Islands?'

'What about them?'

'We can't afford a flight for Whippy and the islands.'

'We'll leave the islands then.'

The Greek Islands disappeared like mist before the sun. It wasn't much of a contest really. Whippy won hands down.

A week before we were due to leave the cottage, Penny invited us to a birthday party at her brother's home. We were fascinated to discover that the house was surrounded by a moat. Parking in the garden, we crossed the wooden bridge over the moat on foot. The house, an old mansion, had huge wooden beams set in the ceilings. A narrow winding staircase led upstairs and some of the rooms were accessible through concealed doors.

There was music and dancing and Russell came over to ask me for a dance. As we danced, he said, 'You almost landed me in a lot of trouble.'

'Me? How on earth did I do that?'

'Moles.'

'Moles? Ah, so it *was* you! You asked your neighbour to poison them!'

'Chrystal, they're pushing up mounds of earth all over the place.'

'Russell, I've a good mind to tell Penny.' I glanced around as if looking for her.

'No . . . no!' he blurted hastily, almost placing his hand over my mouth. 'Don't say anything, please. It'll lead to a divorce.'

'How could you? It's like Watership Down, only with moles.'

I launched into a lurid description of what it would be like for a family of moles if poison gas was pumped into their home. When the music finished Russell, looking shaken, went off to pour himself a drink. But not before I had extracted a promise that he would never lift a finger against a mole again.

'If you don't promise, I'll tell Penny.'

'I promise, I promise!'

It was with sadness that we said goodbye to Penny and Russell and the cottage, knowing that the two long weeks before our flight were going to be traumatic. Whippy had to go into kennels at the animal travel agency, while we went to London to sell the Combi and sort out travel arrangements. With her phobia about being separated from us, we knew it wouldn't be easy.

When we arrived at the kennels, the staff were extremely

kind. Two young women made a fuss of Whippy and assured us that they would give her lots of love. The desolate look in her eyes as we walked away and left her was enough to break our hearts. Sobbing bitterly, we pulled off in the Combi and cried all the way to London.

We discovered to our dismay that our flight home involved a stopover in Luxemburg for several hours. We contacted the animal travel agency immediately and it was decided that Whippy would be booked on to a British Airways flight which flew direct to Johannesburg. Unfortunately it meant that we would arrive in Johannesburg around 8.30 in the morning, whereas Whippy's flight would only land at midday. Also, the time of our departure from Heathrow and Whippy's arrival there did not coincide and we were forced to accept that we would not be able to see her before we boarded.

The day of our departure finally arrived. When we landed at Luxemburg Airport, we were informed that a bus tour and lunch had been arranged to pass the time until our connecting flight was due.

As the tour bus wound its way along narrow country roads, my eyes flicked over the scenic beauty with total disinterest. As far as I was concerned, we may as well have been viewing coal dumps. There was only one thing on my mind. Whippy. Was she all right? She must be so confused, I thought. While we were in London Dave had telephoned the kennels every few days. Whippy was fine, they had assured him, just a bit subdued.

'Subdued? Whippy?' I gazed at Dave in disbelief.

'Chrystal, you must understand that Whippy doesn't know why she's been left there. She most probably thinks we've abandoned her.'

'I wish you wouldn't say things like that.'

'It's the truth. Just remember, the last time she landed in a cage, she stayed there for eight months.'

Dave's sister Erica and her husband Jonathan were at the airport to meet us in Johannesburg. They took us to their home where we planned to spend a few days before flying to my home in the Eastern Cape.

'What time is it?'

'It's 12.15.'

'She should have landed by now.'

'Yes.'

A South African pet travel agency had been commissioned to collect Whippy from the airport and deliver her to Erica's home. The crate was too large to transport in an ordinary vehicle.

Dave and I paced the front garden, peering down the street at intervals. We were exhausted after the long tedious flight, but neither of us could rest until Whippy was with us.

And then we saw it. A large green and white van driving slowly in our direction. We waved and the driver pulled in on to the grass verge.

'There are some papers I need you to sign,' he said, climbing down from the van.

'May we see our dog first?'

'Yes, of course.'

He and Dave opened the rear doors of the van and climbed in. They lifted the crate down and placed it on the grass. Not a sound emerged. My heart was thumping and I wondered if she was alive.

As the crate touched the grass, I bent down and drew the double bolts and the door swung open. There was a moment's silence as Whippy blinked in the sudden light and then she saw me. With a steam-engine shriek of delight, she hurtled out on to the grass, almost bowling me over. She went mad. A whirling dervish of joy and love leapt up at me and then Dave and then me and then Dave again.

After a while the driver became restless.

'Errm, could you sign the papers for me now?'

'Yes, of course, I'm sorry.'

While Dave signed, Whippy jumped up at the driver and, just for good measure, gave his face a few lavish licks. He didn't seem to mind.

For the rest of that day, and in the days that followed, Whippy stuck to us like a leech. Determined that we would not slip off and leave her again, she watched our every move. After three days in the Johannesburg sunlight her bedsores, which we had battled with for so long, began to heal.

We had been in the Eastern Cape for just a few days.

A tan object was hurtling down the beach towards us. Then for an instant it veered off the sand and into the foaming waves. Sparkles of water were flung upwards, catching the sunlight like bright jewels.

Whippy bounced from the sea, shaking herself joyously and scattering water all over us.

She was home.

The Landlady and Old Lace

After we returned from Britain we spent some time with our parents, alternating between their two homes. My father hadn't been well for some months and I was extremely worried about him. Fortunately Dave's parents, Dodo and Bill, lived in a coastal town only an hour's drive from my parents' home.

Dave's German Shepherd Mandy, who had stayed with his friends Roger and Gail in Cape Town while he was overseas, joined us. It didn't take me long to discover that Mandy had dedicated her life to protecting Dave. He was her hero, her *raison d'être*. She approved of Whippy and me, but we knew that if we ever found ourselves in a dangerous situation, she would rescue Dave first. We would have to take our chances.

We set a date for our wedding, and in the meantime Dave made himself available for locums. We purchased a second-hand bakkie. Sturdy and reliable, it was light-blue with a white canopy and in between locums we traversed the country in it. Sometimes we stopped overnight in the middle of nowhere and Dave and I and the two dogs would sleep in the back. There was just enough room for the four of us. Despite its humble appearance, the bakkie bestowed upon us the freedom of the countryside. No longer limited by having to book accommodation in advance or obtain permission for the dogs, we could go anywhere. And we did.

We camped overnight in places of indescribable beauty, isolated, wild and free. On cold nights, packed like four sardines in the back of the vehicle, we'd be lulled to sleep by the keening sounds of the bush or the sighing ocean. If the air was warm, we'd bed down next to the fire. Over the weeks Whippy had reluctantly come to accept that she and I could not fit into one sleeping bag. I'd make a bed out of folded blankets for her at my side, pretending not to notice her reproachful stare.

'Maybe we should buy a double sleeping bag,' I said to Dave.

'For you and me?'

'No. For Whippy and me.'

Mandy slept at Dave's feet, the protector, always on the alert for any sign of danger.

After a locum in Natal, Dave arrived home with Sally, an elderly Corgi. She had been attacked by her owners' new dog, a Rottweiler, and they no longer wanted her. After thirteen years she had become a disposable item. Out with the old and in with the new. They requested euthanasia and Dave refused. He offered to take her.

'She can live out her last golden years with us,' he told them.

Sally was a gracious old lady. One could picture her presiding over tea, handing out cucumber sandwiches and *petits fours*. However, on being introduced to her new family she underwent an instant metamorphosis. Cucumber sandwiches and *petits fours* were tossed from the window as she joined in the rough and tumble of our lifestyle. Dignity thrown to the winds, she discovered the joys of running on the beach, frolicking in the shallows and rolling in the sand.

Shortly before our wedding, Whippy came into season. We had been expecting this and had already made enquiries about male greyhounds in our area. There was only one.

He was black and white and very bombastic and Whippy refused to have anything to do with him.

'*He's too arrogant, I don't like him.*'

'Can't you just pretend to like him?'

'*I don't think so.*'

A few days later she fell hopelessly in love. We were passing through a small town on our way to Dave's parents. As we slowed down at an intersection, a large whippet floated across the road. He was obviously deep in thought.

'*Look at that!*' breathed Whippy reverently.

We looked. He was pearly white with splashes of silver-grey. He had soppy eyes. Like kerb-crawlers up to no good, we inched after him as he led us into a street lined with beautiful old trees. Halfway down the street he turned off into a garden.

Dave ventured forth and knocked on the door of the house. He discovered that the dog's name was Spokie and he belonged to a dentist and his wife. Dr van der Merwe was thrilled at our request. But not half as thrilled as Whippy and Spokie. The romantic interlude lasted a week, with Spokie writing poetry in his head and Whippy swooning into his arms at every opportunity.

Finally, the day of our wedding arrived. Roger and Gail travelled down from Cape Town. Roger was to be Dave's bestman, while my cousin Carmen was my bridesmaid. Whippy and Mandy, their collars bedecked with pink ribbons, sat in the back pew of the church with Gail while we exchanged vows. The reception was to be held at a local hotel and Dave had requested a special platter of sausages for the two dogs.

The steaming platter of sausages was placed on the main table as the guests gathered, but when we arrived with the two dogs it was empty.

'Where are the dogs' sausages?' Dave asked, staring down at the empty plate.

Ivy, an old workmate of mine, paused in the act of licking her fingers. 'What sausages?' she asked.

'The sausages for the dogs. I specifically asked that they be ready when we arrived.'

'Oh no!' she exclaimed.

'What's the matter?' I asked.

'Chrystal, we've eaten them. We've eaten the dogs' sausages.'

As we stared at each other, several guests in the immediate vicinity moved off hastily. Whippy gazed up at Ivy reproachfully and Dave hurried off to order a second platter.

'I've never been so embarrassed in all my life!' Ivy wailed.

'Not to worry, I'm sure they were perfectly edible,' I reassured her.

For our honeymoon, we had booked a small cottage overlooking the beach just outside Dolphin Bay, where Dodo and Bill lived. Mandy, Whippy and Sally came with us.

On our second night there a tremendous storm broke. Lightning flashed across the sky throughout the night, illuminating the bedroom, while the thunder boomed and rolled over the house. Heavy drops of rain pounded on the roof.

Very early the next morning I awoke to the sound of the sea. It was loud, as if waves were breaking in the room with us. After a while, I rose and walked over to the window. An amazing sight met my eyes. Waves were breaking on the grassy area which lay between the cottage and the beach. The beach was gone! In its place lay a surging sea of choppy waves. Huge mounds of creamy white foam had been pushed up on to the grass, like heaps of dirty snow.

'Dave, Dave, wake up! The sea is here!' I shook his sleeping form.

'What do you mean? I know we're at the sea,' he protested sleepily.

'No, no, it's here. Just a few metres from the cottage.'

He got up reluctantly, and as we stood gazing at the scene there was a knock on the front door. It was a policeman. He informed us that the river which lay at the entrance to the small village had come down in flood, preventing vehicles from entering or leaving. We were cut off.

'What about the sea?' I asked nervously. 'If it rises any further the whole village will be under water.'

'Madam, if that should happen, we have helicopters standing by to evacuate the inhabitants.'

'What about the dogs?' I asked Dave anxiously, when the policeman had departed. 'We can't leave without the dogs.'

We spent the rest of the day working out how two people could carry three dogs in their arms, while being hoisted into a helicopter. That night sleep did not come easily and we took turns peering out into the darkness, trying to see whether the waves were any closer.

When dawn finally arrived we were relieved to see that the sea had retreated, leaving the beach covered in waist-high foam. After breakfast we ventured out on to the beach. Whippy and Mandy raced into the foam, only their heads visible as they cavorted and played. Sally, with her short legs, disappeared underneath it and Dave picked her up hastily, fearing that she would be lost in this weird and wonderful landscape.

By late afternoon the foam had melted and a beach that resembled a ravaged moonscape emerged. Uprooted trees, bits of furniture and crayfish traps lay scattered on the shore, thick ropes of seaweed draped over them. We found turtles amongst the debris, some dead, others still alive. We collected the live ones and placed them in the lagoon, hoping that all they needed was rest.

Every day we walked for miles along the beach, entranced by its treasures, collecting driftwood and huge shells cast up from the ocean depths. Before we knew it, the week was at an end and, with it, our honeymoon.

When we returned to my parents' home it was to find that my father had been admitted to hospital earlier that day. Five weeks later he passed away. In trying to come to terms with his death, I found some small consolation in the fact that he had been able to attend our wedding and share in that happiness.

One week later Whippy went into labour and gave birth to nine puppies. In a way, the puppies took our minds off our grief. Four of them were a golden tan colour and the other five were white with silver-grey splotches. They all had soppy eyes.

A few weeks after their birth, Dave was approached by a vet in the Western Cape to do a locum for him. Dr Smith had booked a three-week overseas holiday. Owing to unforeseen circumstances, the locum he had engaged had let him down at the eleventh hour. Dave explained about Whippy and the puppies, but Dr Smith assured him that he would arrange accommodation where dogs and puppies were welcome.

'No problem, no problem,' he said jovially. He was a desperate man.

We packed our suitcases into the back of the bakkie, laying a foam mattress on top of them. Sally, Mandy, Whippy and the puppies curled up comfortably on this bed from which they could look out through the canopy windows.

We arrived in Cape Town late on a Saturday afternoon and spent the night with Roger and Gail. They lived on a smallholding in Hout Bay where they ran a plant nursery. It was a magical place, bordered by a stream deep enough to swim in. We spent the Sunday morning at the stream, swimming in the icy water and lazing in the weak winter sunlight.

The accommodation which Dr Smith had arranged for us was a furnished house in a coastal town, just fifteen minutes' drive from his practice. He had given Dave directions and we agreed to meet the landlady/owner at the house at 5 o'clock on the Sunday afternoon. Apparently she spent weekends in a flat on the same property, but lived elsewhere during the week.

We left Hout Bay just before 4 o'clock. It was winter and when we arrived at the house it was already dusk and streetlights glowed in the misty sea air. After parking the bakkie on the grass verge outside, Dave disappeared through the gate. Five minutes later he returned, accompanied by a tall, thickset woman with iron-grey hair. She swept after him like a ship in full sail and I felt a trickle of unease shimmy down my spine.

As she approached the bakkie Mandy barked. The woman came to an abrupt halt, lips wrinkling in disapproval.

'Oh, you haf a dog?' She was Dutch.

Dave and I stared at each other, appalled. In that split second, I wondered whether we could conceal nine puppies for three weeks? The answer was a firm 'No'.

'Did Dr Smith not mention the dogs and the puppies?' I asked with a weak smile.

'Puppies . . . you haf PUPPIES also?' An expression of disgust flitted across her face, as if I had said 'The Plague' instead of 'Puppies'.

'How many puppies haf you?'

'Nine.'

'NEIN PUPPIES!' she puffed incredulously.

'Yes, Dr Smith was supposed to clear it with you.'

'Dr Smith said nothing, *nothing*, about dogs and puppies . . . NEIN PUPPIES!'

It was a very tricky situation. Dr Smith had already left the country and despite the fact that he had placed us in this awkward position, we were reluctant to let him down.

'Perhaps you could show us over the house,' I said, wondering about Persian carpets and family heirlooms.

She trundled ahead, shaking her head at intervals, muttering foreign words under her breath. I thought I heard '*Mein Gott*', but I couldn't have, that's German. Trailing after her, I suspected that only years of Dutch discipline prevented her from having hysterics right there in front of us.

The kitchen, bathroom and shower room floors were tiled throughout. The remainder of the house had wooden floors. There were no carpets. Fortunately.

'We could pen off an area in the shower,' I suggested. 'It's a big room and easy to clean. The puppies could sleep there at night.'

At the rear of the house was a large, smooth concrete-floored veranda where they could spend their days, when not out on the lawn.

Finally the landlady left, after a long soul-wrenching look at the house. As if she was memorising it. She said she would see us the following weekend.

This was a very inauspicious start to a locum. And it got worse. A few days into the locum, the receptionist ushered a lady carrying a cat basket into the consulting room.

Dave looked up. 'Good morning . . . er . . . Mrs?'

'Mrs Charles, from the local SPCA. I have a cat for euthanasia.'

'Oh, is it ill?'

'Yes, it's in a terrible state.'

'OK, let me see it.'

'You don't have to examine it,' she said haughtily. 'Merely euthanase it.' '

'I'd prefer to examine it first,' he said firmly.

As Dave opened the basket, a beautiful grey and white tabby emerged. Her coat was a bit dirty but apart from that she appeared healthy. Peering into her mouth, he exclaimed, 'Ah, this is why she looks scruffy. See, there is a small cut on the tongue. With treatment this will heal in no time and she'll be licking and cleaning herself again.'

'I'm afraid it must be euthanased.'

'Why? This isn't a serious problem.'

'We do not have a cage for it.'

'Can't you make a plan?'

'I'm afraid not,' she said coldly. 'Dr Smith always euthanases at our request. I'm sure that, as his locum, he would expect you to do the same.' Leaving the cat on the table, she stalked out of the room.

Dave told me later that he stood and stared at the cat for a long time. She was purring. Then, after a while, he drew up the euthanase. She sat perfectly still for him as he injected into the vein. As she slumped down and stopped breathing, the door of the consulting room burst open and a woman rushed in.

'I'm from the SPCA,' she said breathlessly and then she

noticed the dead cat.

'Oh no! We did have a cage for it after all,' she exclaimed in dismay.

Dave looked at her for a moment. Then he turned and left the room without speaking. It was his birthday that day.

When he came home that night he was very quiet and I could sense something was wrong. I had prepared a special meal for his birthday. But he picked at his food, saying he wasn't really hungry. After a while he told me about the cat. We sat at the table in the kitchen and talked for hours.

'If you ever feel strongly that an animal must not be euthanased, then just refuse to do it.'

'It's difficult when it's not your own practice.'

'I know it's tricky but, even so, I think you should just refuse.'

'Chrystal, what would I have done with the cat?'

'You could've brought it here. We can always make a plan. I don't think you should euthanase a healthy animal when you feel so deeply that it's wrong. It affects you too much.'

I could not have foreseen how quickly those words would come back to haunt me. The decisions we took that night were to have a profound effect upon both our lives.

The landlady was keeping us on our toes, having arrived unexpectedly on two occasions in the first week, very early in the morning. So even earlier in the morning I was up and at the shower room with bucket and brush. I don't want to philosophise about puppy pooh, but a little bit goes a long way. Very much like Whippy with her happiness, they had a tendency to spread it around.

On one occasion the landlady arrived with her granddaughter. The child was thrilled to see the puppies who were playing on the lawn and raced around the grass with them to cries of, 'Be careful, don't tramp in that!' from the grand-mother.

Short of walking after them with a shovel, I could do no more.

It was a large house, but I thought it best to close off everything except our bedroom, the passage, kitchen and bathroom, all of which I kept spotlessly clean. I cleaned the shower cubicle every morning, and I rinsed off the veranda two to three times a day. The house was cleaner than it had been when we moved in.

The house was only one block from the beach and initially we had thought this would be marvellous for the three dogs. A couple of days after we arrived we took Mandy, Whippy and Sally to the beach. A nasty surprise awaited us. NO DOGS ALLOWED signs were scattered at intervals and regretfully we were forced to abandon the walk. We returned to the house with three rather morose dogs. It was a built-up area and there was really nowhere else to walk them.

'Maybe we should go very early in the morning,' I suggested.

So on our first Sunday there, at 6 o'clock in the morning, we decided to take the chance.

The beach was deserted. The three dogs were ecstatic at being able to race along the sand, plunging enthusiastically in and out of the sparkling waves. Especially Whippy. She had embraced the South African way of life with open arms.

On our way back she raced off to greet a man approaching us from the opposite direction. He was wearing a khaki-coloured uniform.

'Oh dear,' I said to Dave.

'What?'

'Look!'

Whippy was jumping up joyously at the policeman. Licking him lovingly, she led him straight back to us.

'*Come and meet my family,*' she was saying proudly, as we watched his approach with foreboding. Grim-faced and unsmiling, he took an official-looking notepad from his pocket. And then a pen. Narrowing his eyes, he glared at us.

'You know that dogs are not allowed on this beach?'

'Yes, we knew, but we thought it would be all right if we came very early,' I explained.

'Ah . . . so you *knew*?'

'Yes, but the dogs needed a walk so badly.'

'Madam, the sign clearly states NO DOGS ALLOWED.'

'Yes, but . . .'

'I am afraid I am going to have to fine you.'

'Yes.'

'Name . . .?'

He fined us fifty rands which had to be paid at the nearest police station. Whippy seemed very downhearted as we left the beach.

'I've told you before, never speak to strangers,' I said.

'*I'm sorry, I didn't know he was a policeman. In Britain they wear blue.*'

'You led him right to us.'

'Anyway, I'm not paying it,' Dave stated categorically. 'It's discrimination.'

The next day, Monday, Dave telephoned me.

'Two healthy cats have been brought in to be euthanased.'

'Why?'

'I'm not sure. They were brought in by a Mrs Oakley and

49

her two teenage daughters. They're adamant that they do not want the cats any longer and they won't give me a reason. The one had love-bites all over her neck.'

'Which one?'

'What do you mean, which one?'

'Which cat has love-bites all over its neck?'

'Not the cat. The daughter.'

'Oh.'

'What shall I do?'

'Bring them home.'

'Are you sure?'

'Mmm . . . just bring them. We can try and find homes for them.'

Deep in thought, I replaced the receiver. The only problem I could foresee was the landlady, bless her soul. Dave and I had started referring to her as the Dragon-Lady. This was a bit unfair. Show me a landlady who will welcome three dogs and nine puppies and I'll show you the Holy Grail.

She was still having difficulty coming to terms with the dogs and I was reluctant to tip her over the edge with two cats. Certainly, to conceal nine puppies would have been an impossible task, but two cats? Two little old cats? I went out and bought a litter tray.

All we had to do was close them in our bedroom when she was around. Draw the curtains and nobody would be the wiser.

And so that evening the two cats joined us. They were beautiful. Both were long-haired – one was ginger with a few splashes of white, and the other was a mottled grey tabby with a white bib and white feet. A bit on the thin side, they were uncastrated males. During the course of the day, Dave had castrated them to nip any spraying in the bud. We assumed they were brothers and estimated that they were approximately one year old. They didn't have names.

'What kind of people don't name their cats?' I asked him.

One look at the ginger one and I knew his name was Carrots. Dave wanted to call the grey tabby Brinjal.

'He's not a Brinjal.'

'Why not?'

'He just isn't.'

'What is he then?'

'He's a Philby.'

At the time I was reading a book about Kim Philby, the famous British spy.

I often marvel at the fact that I named Philby so aptly. Had I noticed the sparkle of intrigue in those bright green eyes, on the very first day? Or, having been given the name, did he then decide to live up to it? Later, with hindsight, I realised that he should've had two names. Philby Machiavelli.

Carrots was simply Carrots. He was Philby's sidekick. The fall-guy. Naively, he believed everything Philby told him. And his purring had gears. In top gear he was capable of keeping a household of people awake at night. The two were very different. Incidents that would stimulate Philby would frighten the fur off Carrots.

Disaster struck the second day they were there. As I was coming into the house from the garden I heard distressed meowing from our bedroom. I rushed in and found Carrots dangling from the curtains, his claws hooked in the lace. At a glance I could see the curtains were a write-off, with great big gaping holes in them. As I detached Carrots, I looked around for Philby. He was sitting smugly on the bed, watching me scold Carrots. His face bore a round-eyed expression of total innocence.

'*I told him to leave them alone,*' he smirked.

Then I noticed the tufts of lace between his toes.

This was very awkward. How was I going to explain the tattered lace curtains to the landlady without admitting to the presence of the two cats? Obviously we would have to replace the curtains, there was no question about that. But what could I tell her?

Various explanations flitted through my mind. Dave had tripped and grabbed on to them as he fell . . . Cape vultures had attacked them from outside when the windows were open. But I was forced to dismiss these ideas because, really, when you looked at the curtains you thought CATS.

The second week of the locum was coming to an end. It was Sunday and we were expecting the landlady.

Early that morning, after closing the two cats in our bedroom, we drew the curtains (not the lace ones, they were concealed deep in a cupboard) and went off to buy the Sunday newspapers.

On our return we noticed the landlady's car parked at the front of the house. As we entered the front gate, my heart sank. Standing at our bedroom window with fixed stares on their faces, were the landlady, her daughter and her two granddaughters. Sitting proudly on the inside window sill between the glass and the curtains, were Carrots and Philby. Both groups seemed equally mesmerised.

As the gate creaked shut, she turned and spotted us and her face appeared to go into a spasm.

After a moment's difficulty, she hissed, 'What are *those*?'

How could I answer the question? Anyone could see they were cats.

And to eradicate any further doubt, Philby was shouting raucously, *'We're CATS, lady . . . and we LIVE here.'*

He had a few rough edges in those early days.

Unfortunately the situation deteriorated even further

when I turned to the two children and said brightly, 'Wouldn't you like to have a cat?'

They nodded eagerly but before I could pursue this possibility, their grandmother had gripped them by their hands and dragged them around the back of the house to the flat.

Later that morning she knocked on the front door and asked if she could get something from one of the bedrooms. She never mentioned the cats. So I didn't either. There is a time to speak and a time to keep quiet. She left later that afternoon. At eight o'clock that night the telephone rang.

'Mrs Sharp, tomorrow is the end of the month and I want you people out of the house by twelve noon.'

'Twelve noon tomorrow!' I exclaimed. 'But what about my husband's locum? Dr Smith booked the house for three weeks.'

'There must haf been some misunderstanding. I haf udder people coming in the day after tomorrow.'

'But what are we going to do? My husband still has another week to work!'

'Zat is not my problem. And the house smells musty.'

'That's because all the rooms have been closed for two weeks. We're only using the bedroom, kitchen and bathroom.'

'Twelve noon,' she said firmly, slamming the phone down.

I went to find Dave. 'That was the landlady. She wants us out of the house by 12 o'clock tomorrow.'

'Why?'

'She says the house smells musty.'

'But Dr Smith booked the house for three weeks.'

'I know that.'

'What are we going to do?'

Dave phoned Roger and Gail. They said we must spend

the week with them. The only snag was that Dave would have an hour's drive to and from the practice each day. And what was worse, he would have to repeat this if any after-hours emergencies arose.

We sat down at the kitchen table and worked out a plan for the next day. We decided that Dave would help me load the bakkie early the next morning. I would set off for Hout Bay with the dogs, puppies and cats, while he, having the practice vehicle, would go to work. He'd return to the house at twelve to hand over the keys and pay for the lace curtains.

Most of the night was spent packing and cleaning. Well after midnight, I broached a subject that had been worrying me.

'How am I going to find my way to Cape Town?'

'What do you mean?'

'I don't know the way to Cape Town.'

'Surely you remember the way we came?'

'Not really.'

'I'll draw you a map.'

He drew me a map in the finest detail. It began at the house. There were stop signs, left-hand turns, right-hand turns, yield signs, slipways and even landmarks. It was a work of art.

One of my many failings is that I lack a sense of direction. This is not a philosophical statement about my life. I literally lack a sense of direction. My eyes take in the surroundings, not the actual route. Like bits of a puzzle, each familiar area stands alone. I am incapable of fitting them together. For me, getting lost is as easy as leaving a shop by a different door from the one through which I entered. As far as I was concerned, travelling *to* Cape Town was entirely different to travelling *from* Cape Town by the same route. Everything would be in reverse.

Just Another Day in Paradise

Very early the next morning we packed the bakkie, laying the foam mattresses on top of our cases. Whippy, Mandy, Sally and the nine pups would travel in the back, while Philby and Carrots would be in front with me. Although it was early, the day was already showing signs of becoming hot. Fortunately, my estimated time of arrival in Hout Bay was just after nine, well before the heat set in.

With a kiss and a wave I pulled out into the street with the map on the seat next to me. Philby perched on the backrest behind my head while Carrots huddled on my lap, slightly uneasy but quiet. According to the map, at the first stop sign after leaving town I should turn right.

As I approached the stop sign, I noticed a huge signboard lying on the ground surrounded by road workers. Craning my neck, I tried to read it, but it was tilted away from me. Not to worry, I thought, I don't need the sign, I have the map. I turned right and drove on.

On either side of the road there were clumps of trees, with cool areas of shade beneath them, scattered amidst lush pastures, bright green after the winter rains. Here and there a farmhouse nestled on a hill. So restful and rustic, I thought. Eyes drinking in the peaceful green surroundings, I sang softly to myself, *'All around the purple heather . . .'* I passed two men working on the road and waved a greeting. They waved back.

It was after about thirty minutes that the first element of doubt crept in. If this countryside was so beautiful, why hadn't I noticed it on our way from Cape Town? I could not recall this type of scenery on that trip, remembering only a two-lane motorway bordered by scrubland. I pulled to the side of the road and examined the map carefully. No doubt about it, I had followed Dave's instructions to the last letter. But where was the motorway? After giving the matter some thought, I decided to turn back and see if I had missed a signpost somewhere. Driving slowly, I examined the route for signboards, but could see none, only boards with farm names. As I passed the two road workers, I waved again and they waved back, looking slightly puzzled.

'*We're lost,*' Philby confided to Carrots.

'We're *not* lost.' I said firmly. 'We're just uncertain.'

Now the second element of doubt crept in. You're being silly, I thought, you should've just kept going. More than likely the entrance to the motorway is just around the corner from where you turned back. Relieved at having come to this conclusion, I made a U-turn and drove back along the road. This time, as I flashed past them, the two road workers leaned on their shovels and stared after me.

Eventually, I passed the spot where I had stopped and turned. There was no sign of a motorway around the next bend. Or the next. Just farmland and countryside.

My appreciation of the scenic beauty was evaporating rapidly as the first ripples of stress kicked in. I stopped singing. The kilometres slipped by. Glancing at my watch, I saw that it was almost two hours since I had left the house. Two hours and still no motorway! This is no good, I thought, I'll have to stop and ask someone. The only living souls I had seen were the two road workers. So, yet again, I made a U-turn.

'*We're definitely lost,*' Philby informed Carrots, from his vantage point behind my head.

I pretended not to hear.

As the two men watched the bakkie approach, they stopped digging and put down their shovels. They appeared to be rigid with curiosity. One began scratching his head. I pulled over, climbed from the bakkie and walked up to them, map in hand.

'Good morning,' I said, feeling slightly embarrassed.

'Morning . . . morning,' they chorused, nodding their heads vigorously. And then they waited.

'I'm trying to get to Cape Town.'

'*Cape Town*? . . . but Ma'am won't get to Cape Town on this road. This isn't the road to Cape Town.'

'Hmmm, I thought not. You see, my husband drew me this map.'

I handed them the map. They examined it in silence, totally absorbed. After a while I cleared my throat. I pointed at the map: 'This is where I started from . . . and this is where I turned right.'

They nodded thoughtfully. Then one said, 'But Ma'am, your husband has drawn you the long way to Cape Town, I'll show you the short way.'

'No,' I said hastily, reluctant to become involved with a new set of directions. 'Don't worry about the short way, just show me the right long way.'

'But Ma'am, the short way is *much* quicker.'

'I'm sorry, I can't go the short way,' I said firmly. 'My husband took a lot of trouble with this map.'

Heaven only knows what they thought of this explanation but I had reached the stage where I no longer cared.

They showed me how to get on to the motorway. It was very simple really. The map may have been a work of art, but it was missing one stop sign. I should've turned right at the second stop sign after leaving town.

Thanking them profusely, I set off once again. On my way back I passed the signboard which had been lying on the ground. Workers were now busy erecting it. It said STELLENBOSCH. Oh well.

Within five minutes I was on the motorway, sweating as the heat shimmered above the tar. Sensing my agitation, Philby and Carrots began meowing. As I stroked them soothingly, their fur stuck to my hands, and as I wiped my sweating brow it was transferred to my face. Soon my face was covered in cat fur, which began tickling my nostrils. I started to sneeze violently. Then I glanced in the rear view mirror to check on the dogs and my heart skipped a beat. One of the windows in the canopy was wide open. The window was level with the mattress. Oh dear God! What if one of the puppies had fallen out?

Screeching to a halt alongside the road, I sprang out of the bakkie. Heart pounding, I opened the canopy and started counting. One-two-three-four-five-six-seven ... SEVEN! Oh no! One-two-three-four-five-six-seven-eight-nine-ten. Well, it couldn't be ten, there were only nine puppies. The trouble with greyhound/whippet puppies is that they move so fast that it is extremely difficult to count them.

On my third attempt, I arrived at nine. Just to be sure, I did a recount, and then another. Closing the window and the canopy, I climbed back in behind the wheel. Would this journey never end, I wondered wearily?

Philby and Carrots were hot and panting now and they draped themselves over my lap, both clasping the steering-wheel. As I entered Cape Town, I immediately encountered heavy traffic. The map became more complex, with a right turn here and a left turn there. Referring to it constantly, I struggled to read street names through spectacles which were plastered with cat fur. Each time I turned right, Carrots would be pulled upwards as if he was on a big wheel at a fairground, only to drop to the floor with a thud as his grip weakened. When I turned left it was Philby's turn. As I nudged them away from the pedals with my feet, they would claw their way back to my lap and the whole process would start again.

Just before midday, after being on the road for almost four hours, I turned into Roger and Gail's driveway. I switched off the ignition and sat staring vacantly into space. I think I might still have been there if Roger hadn't arrived on the scene.

'Chrystal, are you all right?'

'Yes, I'm fine.'

The house was some distance from the driveway with greenhouses and plant beds in between. Climbing wearily from the bakkie, I realised I could not allow nine bounding puppies to run in nine different directions through the greenhouses and plant beds. I would have to carry them to the house.

But first I would take Philby and close him in our bedroom and then I would return for Carrots. I checked the windows. They were all closed. But ten minutes later when I returned with Carrots, I discovered, to my dismay, that Philby was no longer in the room. Where on earth could he be? Desperately I searched under beds and behind cupboards. Then I found his escape route: a broken window pane hiding slyly behind a curtain.

This was too much. The floodgates opened and the tears streamed down as I sat on the bed with Carrots on my lap, weeping noisily.

'Hoooo . . . hoo . . . Carrots, your brother's gone . . . we'll never see him again . . . hoooo . . . '

Carrots was handling it quite well, I noticed. Apart from a slight uneasiness because my tears were dripping on to his fur, he seemed to accept the loss of his brother quite stoically.

Eventually I pulled myself together. I stuffed newspaper into the broken pane and staggered back to the bakkie to begin ferrying the puppies to the house. They were quite big now and I could carry only two at a time. I left the fattest one for last and I carried him alone. His name was Strider. By the time I had made five trips to and from the bakkie, my name felt like Strider too.

I spent the afternoon combing the area and calling 'PHILBY . . . PHILBEEEE!' At half past five there was still no sign of him. I sat down disconsolately on a rock next to the stream and stared at the ground. How was I going to break the news to Dave? Sighing heavily, I looked up.

Across the stream, on the opposite bank, sat Philby. For a few seconds we stared at each other expressionlessly.

Then I burst out, 'You little s..t . . . WHERE HAVE YOU BEEN?'

'*Oh, here and there . . . exploring.*'

'I'll give you exploring! I've spent the whole afternoon searching for you.'

'*But why? I wasn't lost.*'

'You come over here. This minute.'

'*I can't . . . I'll get my feet wet.*'

Fully clothed, I waded through the thigh-deep water to the other side and, bundling him in my arms, I waded back. Wet and cold, I made my way up to the house and shoved him into the bedroom.

As I pulled the door shut, I heard him say to Carrots, '*I don't know what all the fuss is about.*'

A Split Infinitive

I noticed the box when I entered the room to take Dave a cup of tea. It was a small brown cardboard box with a few holes punched into the sides and the flaps secured with twine. Dave, busy writing up a card before seeing the next client, looked up as I came in.

'What's in the box?' I asked curiously.

'Never mind.'

'What do you mean, "Never mind"?'

'It's for euthanasia.'

'What's for euthanasia?'

'A cat. Look Chrystal, I'm busy at the moment.'

'Why must it be euthanased?'

'It's crippled.'

'Oh.'

'And it's pregnant.'

'Oh.'

'And it's wild.'

'Can I look?'

'No! It will just upset you.'

Dave was doing yet another locum, this time in a practice comprising a veterinary hospital in one town and two branch clinics in smaller towns, on the Natal coast. One of the two smaller clinics consisted of a reception area and consulting room in a large old house. We were living in another part of the house. Most of the rooms were completely empty as the house was due to be demolished shortly and the site developed into high-rise flats. The garden was magnificent. As old as the house, it was dominated by four huge frangipani trees. The air was filled with the fragrance of their blossoms, some a creamy white, others a delicate pink. Only in Natal had I ever seen a frangipani so tall.

I was staring down at the box while Dave, shoulders hunched, was ignoring me, when the receptionist popped her head around the door.

'Doctor, the client is experiencing difficulty removing the dog from his vehicle.'

'Is it aggressive?'

'Yes. Apparently it's his wife's dog and she's in hospital.'

'I'm coming,' Dave said, leaving the room hastily, clearly relieved to postpone the matter of the box and its contents.

Following him outside to a police van, I saw the doors at the back were open. Crouched inside was a massive bull-mastiff. Two policemen in uniform were standing at the open doors.

One turned to Dave. 'Sorry, Doc,' he apologised. 'Terror has always been a bit funny with me. My wife is in hospital having our baby and now Terror isn't well.'

I watched apprehensively as Dave clambered into the back of the van. Terror growled deep in his throat as Dave edged nearer and squatted down, speaking soothingly. 'That's a good boy . . . good dog . . . you see, you don't have to be scared.'

He reached out his hand for the dog to sniff and began stroking its head gently. By this time my heart was pumping in my throat.

'Come, my boy,' Dave murmured, picking up the lead

attached to the dog's collar. The dog rose and followed him meekly from the van.

Back in the consulting room the fun began. At first Terror allowed Dave to examine him. He appeared to have a hot spot in the head area. This begins with a small irritated spot on the skin which can spread rapidly over a large area, causing major irritation and discomfort. In order to establish the extent of the spot and treat it effectively, the animal's hair has to be shaved in the specific area.

All went well, until Dave approached with the shaving equipment. Terror decided to call it a day. Enough was enough, he was going home to mommy. With a grunt like a waking giant, he rose from the floor, effortlessly shaking off the two burly policemen who were holding him down. Scattering the shaving equipment in his wake, he lurched for the door. I watched as three grown men tried to restrain one dog, hanging on grimly as he dragged them around the room shaking them off like skittles. This was a dog who was not going to be messed with. I knew what he was thinking. No one was going to shave *his* head. The indignity of it!

Dave, trying desperately to inject a sedative into the moving target, glanced over his shoulder and issued an order. 'Chrystal, I think you should get out of here.'

'OK,' I murmured agreeably. On my way to the door I picked up the cardboard box and nipped out with it tucked under my arm.

I took the box into one of the empty rooms and closed the door. Then I went to fetch a bowl of milk. Returning with the milk, I squatted down next to the box and began untying the twine. As I lifted the flaps and peered inside, a small truculent face gazed back up at me. A scrunched-up raisin of a face that was busy gathering itself for an almighty hiss and spit. The hiss flew past me, breaking the sound-barrier somewhere near the ceiling. This was reinforced by an explosive spit. Then she sat back calmly and waited for my reaction.

I dipped my finger into the milk and very slowly extended it towards her nose. She sniffed the milk tentatively and then a little pink tongue emerged and began to lick my finger. Gently tipping the box on to its side, I placed the bowl of milk slightly away from the opening. With a suspicious glare that warned me not to try anything silly, she emerged cautiously and began lapping the milk. As she drank, I ran my finger softly down her back and she paused, looking over her shoulder at me for a few seconds, before continuing to drink.

She was a cinnamon and grey tabby with a touch of white and she was tiny for an adult cat – stunted and very thin, except for the bulging stomach. Both hind legs were deformed, one shorter than the other. She held the longer leg further away from her body. It seemed to be rigid, not bending at the knee, and as she crouched to drink she appeared to be doing the splits.

When the saucer was empty, she did not creep back into the box as I had expected, but proceeded to carry out an inspection of the room. This was not an exploration, this was an *inspection* and she didn't walk, she marched. One could almost see the baton tucked under the arm. Possibly a military upbringing, I thought as I watched her. Of course, the deformity of her hind legs was responsible for the stiff-legged gait but, as we would discover, her personality was indeed a militant one.

When Dave came to find me, she was cradled in my arms, purring comfortably as I stroked her little body. She tensed when she saw him, but after a perfunctory hiss and spit, she settled back and carried on purring. I could see that she liked to let everyone know where they stood.

'Her name is Splittie.'

'Oh yes?'

'And she's very agile, despite her crippled legs.'

'Mmmmm.'

'Where did she come from?'

'A young couple brought her in. They said she was living wild in the bushes near a restaurant on the beachfront.'

'Crippled and living wild. That couldn't have been easy.'

'No. Apparently she was surviving on scraps of food from the refuse bins. They said she's had kittens before, but dogs got hold of them.'

'Can we keep her?'

'OK.'

Small, stunted and belligerent though she was, to me Splittie was a delight. She bullied the dogs, who quickly developed a very healthy respect for her. If she thought they were out of line, she would scuttle over and paw-whip their faces. Sometimes she was unable to retract her claws and agonised howls would bring us rushing to find Splittie dangling from Whippy's cheek. Poor old Whippy! She suffered the most. It was her nose that got her into trouble every time.

'Why does she always pick on me?'

'Well, you will insist on sniffing her.'

'But I sniff everything.'

'I know that, but she's not used to it.'

Philby and Carrots accepted Splittie quite amicably. Carrots was inclined to be intimidated by her while Philby, true to form, deliberately set out to torment her. Often, as Splittie sat staring into space, deep in thought, he would creep up behind, jump on her and then race off into the distance leaving her spluttering with frustrated rage.

Philby was giving me a hard time. He had disappeared twice during the locum, both times for a day. The first incident occurred just after we arrived. We spent the first few days at the vet's home and on our first night there I closed Philby and Carrots in the games room. The next morning only Carrots was there.

'Where is Philby?' I asked worriedly, having searched the room to no avail.

'He's gone,' Carrots muttered miserably.

'How did he get out?'

'Through there,' he pointed to a narrow opening in the louvred window. *'He wanted me to come too, but I couldn't fit.'*

'Never mind, let me fetch you some breakfast.'

I spent the rest of the day going from house to house in the neighbourhood, asking if anyone had seen a fluffy grey and white striped cat with an exceptionally attractive tail. Making an utter fool of myself really.

At 5.30 that afternoon, still desperately worried, I was standing on the front lawn when I spotted Philby approaching from two houses away. Sauntering over to me, eyes glinting with excitement, he rubbed himself affectionately against my legs.

'Where have you been? I've been worried sick!'

'Oh . . . nowhere really . . . just out.'

'Out where?'

'Oh . . . here and there.'

'Don't ever do that to me again!'

'Did you know that there are two Rottweilers living down the road? And they don't like cats?'

'I've a good mind to give you a hiding!'

'What for? What've I done?'

I scooped him up and locked him in the laundry until the next morning.

Carrots was much fatter than Philby. There was a reason for this. Shortly after we acquired them, we noticed that Philby ate twice as much as Carrots, yet he remained thin. Dave examined him and found that all his lymph glands were enlarged. When we came to Natal, Dave took him to Angus, a colleague whom we both held in very high regard. Angus confirmed Dave's diagnosis. Philby had feline leukaemia. We started him on a course of cytotoxic drugs.

In his swashbuckling way, Philby had conned himself deep into our hearts. All we could do was pray and hope for the best.

A Second Constellation

After a particularly stressful locum, Dave and I returned to my mother's home for a break. During the locum, the vet's own cat had vomited what appeared to be pure acid on to their grand piano. The hours spent trying to remove the stain were interspersed with hours spent spraying fuchsias in hanging baskets.

Dave had not fared much better at the practice and we both felt the need to get away from people for a while. Far away.

Terrence, an old friend of mine, offered to take us hiking up a gorge in a nearby nature reserve. I had been up the gorge before on several occasions.

Terrence and I had grown up together. He was the closest thing to a brother I have ever had.

A few years before, while he was involved in the rehabilitation of injured eagles, Terrence had been exploring an area as a possible release site for the eagles when he came upon the gorge. The entrance to the gorge was concealed by thick bush and tangled curtains of creepers and lay on the far side of a river which was dotted with small islands of reeds. It could be crossed on foot when it was not in full flood.

'Farmers in the area say the gorge is haunted,' Terrence informed me.

'Oh, why would they think that?'

'Their dogs refuse point-blank to venture up it.'

'That's interesting.'

'Hmmm. Tizzy and I are going up the gorge this weekend, you're welcome to come along. It's going to be quite a strenuous hike. Once you enter the gorge you have to walk for about one kilometre upstream.'

'Why upstream?'

'Well, thick undergrowth and forest extend right down to the banks of the stream which runs through the gorge,' he explained. 'It's easier to walk in the water than attempt to force a way through the bush.'

'I don't mind walking upstream, but let me think about it.'

The problem was Tizzy. He and I were barely on speaking terms, after a date arranged by Terrence.

Tizzy had taken me to a party on a farm. During the course of the evening, I glanced up and saw three young men, illuminated by the flickering light of the fire, dancing naked on the roof of an outbuilding. It was a while before I realised that one of the young men was Tizzy. Deeply offended by what I regarded as inappropriate behaviour for a first date, I left.

'How could you let me go on a date with him?' I complained to Terrence the next day. 'He's wild.'

'Well, he's not called The Mad Italian for nothing.'

'What do you mean, "Mad Italian"? You never mentioned a word about a mad Italian.'

'I'm telling you now.'

'Really Terrence, you should've told me before.'

I left in a huff. This was not the action of a brother, I thought bitterly.

Inevitably, the thought of spending two days in the bush proved irresistible and after a brief inner battle, I phoned Terrence.

'I'd like to come.'

'Fine. Tizzy's brother will drop us at the river very early on Saturday. He'll collect us again on Sunday afternoon.'

The sky was still tinged with the pink of dawn as we stood gazing across the river. It was flowing strongly with hummocks of earth and reeds partially submerged.

'It looks a bit deep,' I murmured doubtfully.

'There's been some rain this week.'

'Just remember, you and Tizzy are over six feet tall. I'm only just over five.'

'You'll be fine.'

Terrence entered the water first, followed closely by Tizzy. I watched them for a few seconds and when they were waist-deep I followed. The bottom sloped steeply downwards and in no time water was churning around my chest. Battling to maintain my footing against the strong current, I shrugged off the rucksack and carried it above my head.

As we negotiated our way around small islands and through channels, the water became even deeper and the current kept forcing me sideways. Edging around an island, trying desperately to maintain a toehold, I waded forwards. And sank. Still grasping the rucksack, as my feet touched the bottom, I pushed upwards. My head cleared the water and I shrieked 'HELP!' and promptly sank again. A hand grasped my hair and pulled me to the surface, spluttering and coughing up mouthfuls of river.

'Are you all right?' asked Tizzy, holding me up.

'It's too deep.'

'Hold on to me.'

'Thank you,' I said stiffly, and stared balefully at Terrence who was occupied in observing a heron flying overhead.

'Of course the river is riddled with bilharzia,' Terrence informed us that night, as we squatted around the fire. Tizzy and I stared at him through narrowed eyes.

'That's why I always wear two sets of underpants when crossing it,' he continued.

'What do you mean? Why two sets of underpants?'

'Bilharzia is a microscopic snail which enters the body through any orifice. It proceeds to lay eggs in various organs. The eggs form spines as they grow. They can cause fatal organ damage.'

'Why didn't you mention this before?'

'I'm telling you now. It can be very tricky to treat.'

I spent the rest of that night and the next day worrying about my orifices. As it happened, I needn't have.

When I got home I immediately consulted a medical dictionary. I discovered that bilharzia is caused by a blood fluke or worm which enters the body through the skin. So much for the two sets of underpants, I thought.

The crystal-clear, knee-deep water swirled around my legs. Wading against the flow, I paused for a moment to adjust the straps of my rucksack and to glance briefly at my feet. To check if they were still there. All sensation was long since numbed by the icy water gushing into the stream from the surrounding mountains. As I picked my way cautiously, slipping and sliding on submerged stones and trying to keep Dave and Terrence within sight, the hair on the back of my neck rose.

Right on time, I thought, as I rounded a bend to see the rock-face rising up from the water, jutting out slightly overhead. Advancing warily, I drew level with the rock, my skin crawling as gooseflesh trickled over my body. The colour of fresh blood, the rock loomed over the water like a sinister troll guarding ancient secrets. I was overwhelmed by the sensation of hidden eyes, watching. As I passed and left it behind my back tensed in fear, half expecting a lingering touch.

'Wait for me,' I shouted.

Up ahead, Dave and Terrence stopped and turned.

'I wish you wouldn't leave me to pass the rock on my own,' I muttered crossly to Terrence.

'Sorry.'

On my first encounter with the rock years before, I had known immediately why dogs were wary of the gorge.

When we reached the clearing where we were going to camp the sun had already sunk behind the encircling mountains. We climbed up the steep embankment and set about gathering wood and stones for a fireplace before darkness set in. Later, after supper, we huddled in sleeping bags, our drowsy conversation gradually becoming interspersed with long contented silences. Shifting comfortably in the black sandy soil, its moist smell mingling with the scent of bush, we lay on our backs, staring upwards. Above us, branches and leaves formed a canopy which sheltered us from the night sky. Through gaps in the intertwined silhouettes we could see splashes of dark sky littered with stars.

Suddenly, in the silence, two tiny globes of luminous green light flickered amongst the branches. Two became four. Then ten. Then more.

'Look at that,' Dave whispered, as the fireflies gathered above us in their hundreds.

They seemed to come from nowhere until the branches were illuminated by a deep subterranean-like glow. They flashed on and off, on and off, like strings of twinkling Christmas lights.

Entranced and mesmerised by the magic of this second constellation, we lay in silent wonder below the enchanted gathering, not daring to speak or move for fear they would leave.

Time passed. Gradually they became fewer, the lights moving off into neighbouring trees. Finally there were two. And then none. They had switched off the lights. It was bedtime in the bush.

Our family of animals, like the loaves and fishes, was showing a distinct tendency to divide and multiply.

Like any other average couple we had started our marriage with two dogs, Mandy and Whippy. At my parents' home I had two cats – Blossom, my Siamese, and Nugget, a ginger cat I had rescued as a kitten. So we had two dogs and two cats. A nice even number. Then Sally arrived and Whippy gave birth to the nine puppies. We had wanted her to have a litter because having one Whippy was not enough. We loved her so much that we needed two Whippys – then we could each have one.

When the puppies were born the arguments began. Dave and I could not agree on which one of the puppies we should keep. The dispute dragged on for six weeks. Finally we reached a compromise. We kept two puppies.

Dave's choice was a white and silver-grey female. Shy and soft-natured, she had a grey mark on her head resembling a Bushman arrow. So we called her Arrow. I chose Strider, the large male. Friendly and outgoing, with Whippy's tan colouring, he was magnificent, sleek and shining with muscles that rippled as he moved.

Initially we had tried rather half-heartedly to find homes for Carrots and Philby but after a few weeks we decided that they weren't going anywhere. They belonged with us. Suddenly we had five dogs and four cats, no longer such an even number.

And then Splittie marched into our lives. My mother's home was still our base and shortly after we returned from Natal, Splittie gave birth to two kittens. They were the spitting image of her, two little Splitties. Cosily ensconced in a large drawer, she cleaned them until they squeaked. No longer needing to fight for survival, she relaxed and loved them with all of her battleaxe heart. She even accepted the presence of the dogs in the room, as long as they didn't LOOK.

'*NO EYE CONTACT!*' she would scream, emerging from the drawer like one of Hell's Furies and lashing the offender with a sharp bunch-of-fives. Offender-in-Chief was, of course, Whippy who would dearly have loved kittens of her own.

For some time now, Dave and I had felt the need to set up our own home. Matters finally came to a head when he misplaced a snake in my mother's sitting-room.

Someone had brought him two snakes which had been slightly injured and he placed them in an empty fish tank in a sunny corner of the sitting-room. When my mother queried the need for keeping snakes in the sitting-room, Dave said they had to be there because it was the sunniest room in the house.

What could she say? She had an absolute phobia about snakes, the result of a childhood incident involving one of her brothers and a bath. I'm not sure of the finer details, but I think he threw a live snake into the bath while she was in it. I seem to recall hearing something about her running naked through a house full of people.

Sarah, who was my mother's domestic worker, wasn't happy either. Heavily superstitious, she regarded snakes as something a witch used. To do bad things to you. She refused to clean the room while the snakes were there and so Dave offered to remove the fish tank each day while she cleaned.

'Dave, where's the other snake?' I asked one day.

'What other snake?'

'There were two snakes in here.'

'Yes.'

'Well, now there's only one.'

'It must be under a stone.'

'It's not. I've looked.'

Dave sifted through the sand carefully. There was only one snake. We stared at each other in horror. The missing snake was a red-lipped herald, not highly poisonous but capable of inflicting a painful bite.

Boxes of Dave's veterinary files were stacked in the same corner as the fish tank.

'Should we search the boxes first or the room in general? It'll take us days to go through the files.'

'Let's check the room first. If we don't find it, then we can work through the files.'

'All right.'

A few minutes later, as I was groping under the settee and Dave was on his hands and knees peering under the kist, my mother entered the room.

'What are you looking for?' she asked.

'A book,' I said, with a warning look at Dave.

'Which book? I can help you look.'

'Don't worry, we'll manage.'

She settled into one of the chairs I had not yet searched. Dave and I stared at her nervously.

'Why are you looking at me like that?'

'We're just looking.'

In the days that followed, we watched my mother and Sarah closely. When they were busy in the sitting-room, we were busy in the sitting-room. When they weren't, we searched furtively. Visions of my mother reaching into a desk drawer and grabbing a snake instead of a ruler were constantly with us. Sometimes at night when she was watching TV she would kick off her shoes and Dave and I would watch them anxiously. Snakes like small dark places.

After six nerve-racking days of lurking in the sitting-room, we found the snake. It was in one of the files.

Really, it was time to find a place of our own.

Because he was unable to find a permanent post in the Eastern Cape, Dave applied for a position which had been advertised in Swaziland. We drove to Mbabane for an interview and as we passed through the border post we fell in love with the country. There was an atmosphere of freedom there.

The position was not an assistantship. Veterinary premises and supplies would be provided and the successful applicant would earn a percentage of the professional fees. Neither the vet who was advertising nor ourselves were sure if this system would work, but we decided to give it a try.

We returned home and began packing and making plans. We found a home for one of Splittie's kittens and decided to keep the other, which we called Seafood. We knew that Splittie's love for them was so great that even giving one away was going to cause severe trauma.

She hunted for the second kitten for days. In the end she blamed Whippy.

'*You've taken it, haven't you?*'

'*Taken what?*'

'*My kitten.*'

'*Your kitten? . . . No, I haven't.*'

'*Yes, you have . . . and I'll see that you pay.*'

'*But I don't have your kitten!*'

'*You've sold it then, I suppose.*'

'*But . . .*'

From then on Whippy wasn't even allowed to look at Seafood out of the corner of her eye. If she tried to, it was 'seek and destroy', as Splittie rampaged through the house after her.

With a sore heart, I decided to leave Blossom with my mother. Once we were settled in Swaziland we would make arrangements to fetch him. My most beloved cat, he was not used to travelling and he did not get on very well with Splittie, Philby and Carrots. We felt that if we introduced him after they were established he would be less aggressive towards them.

We decided to take Nuggie with us. Having had a deprived early childhood, he accepted most things with equanimity. Originally I had found him in a box with two other kittens, all of them covered in red ants, and I suspected that after that experience he felt that things could only improve.

Finally the day of our departure arrived. With the bakkie packed to within an inch of its life, we pulled off amidst tears and waves.

A Royal Pain

And so we came to Swaziland, with all our worldly possessions loaded into the back of the bakkie. Also loaded into the bakkie were five dogs, five cats and Dave and me. Fortunately we did not have many worldly possessions, there wouldn't have been space for them.

When Dave accepted the position in Swaziland, a housing agent had taken us to view several houses. The house we decided on was one of a group of prefabricated houses originally built by a road construction company for its employees. The road project had long since been completed and several of the houses were vacant and available to private tenants.

To reach the houses, which were at the bottom of a hill, we turned off the highway leading to Manzini on to a dirt track. After about one kilometre the track wound downhill to the houses – five on either side of the bumpy track. Ours was the first house on the right as you drove in. Directly behind it lay the forest. Beyond the houses opposite ours thick veld and bush stretched as far as the eye could see.

It was a beautiful setting, quiet and wild, and too far from the Manzini road for even the slightest sound of traffic to intrude. The air was rich with the smell of raw red earth mingled with the scent of veld and forest. The front door was on the side of the house facing a ramp of stones set in cement. At the top of the ramp the veld began, tall thick grass and bush. Running along the front of the house was a wide flower bed filled with a profusion of ferns, hen-and-chicks, geraniums and nasturtiums. From the border of the flower bed an area of knee-high grass sloped down to the dirt road. Despite its being a prefab house it was spacious, with three bedrooms, a kitchen, a bathroom and a very large L-shaped lounge.

The veterinary clinic was operated from a mobile home in the centre of Manzini. Two days after we arrived, Dave set off early in the morning, taking Mandy with him.

'I may not be home for lunch,' he said. 'I'll need a bit of time to get myself organised.'

'That's fine.'

I didn't mind. There was a whole new world to explore and it was just outside our door.

When the bakkie had disappeared up the hill, I set off into the forest accompanied by Whippy, Arrow, Strider, Sally and all the cats except Seafood.

'*She's much too young to be roaming a forest,*' Splittie said firmly, when I broached the subject.

As we wandered between the huge tree trunks Philby disappeared up one, only to drop down on Splittie who was stomping along inspecting them for signs of disease. Carrots (who had never had a head for heights) remained firmly on the ground, purring loudly as he oiled himself from one trunk to another. Whippy and Nuggie stayed at my side, while Arrow and Strider dashed off to explore. Sally plodded along behind us. She believed in thorough sniffing at her own pace. None of this hit-and-run sniffing for her.

In some places the undergrowth was thick and impen-etrable, in others a layer of soft faded leaves decked the ground between the trees. We were ambling along peacefully deep in the forest when I suddenly spotted a house through the trees. As we approached I saw that it was a large, rambling, colonial-style house, painted white, with a veranda running along its full length. Bougainvillaea in glorious red, mauve and orange tumbled from the roof of the veranda. The garden wore an air of neglect, shrubs and bushes growing uncontrolled, while flower beds overflowed on to pebbled paths.

I was looking at the house, wondering if anyone lived there, when a short stocky Swazi man appeared from between the trees. Dressed in a dull green combat uniform and carrying a large gun, he stood in front of us, sour-faced, regarding me and the dogs suspiciously. Then his gaze took in the four cats and an expression of disbelief rippled over his face.

Somewhat unnerved, I smiled hesitantly and called out, 'Good morning.'

He grunted. Whippy, overjoyed at meeting yet another new friend, ran up to him, tail wagging in circles. His expression softened as he looked down at her. The Swazis have a great affection for greyhounds. But when he looked up, his expression hardened once more.

'King's house,' he gestured towards the house.

'Oh.'

'Private. Not allowed near King's house.'

'Oh, I'm sorry. I didn't know.'

'No hunting, King's property.'

'Pardon?'

'NO HUNTING.' This time he spat it out.

'I'm not hunting,' I protested indignantly. 'I don't have any weapons.'

'NO HUNTING,' he pointed to the dogs.

'Oh . . . Oh no, they don't hunt, we don't allow them to.'

Another grunt. He tapped his foot on the ground, obviously impatient for us to leave. Calling the cats and dogs to me, I turned back the way we had come. When I glanced back over my shoulder, he was still watching us. I decided that in future I would make sure we stayed well clear of the house.

Arrow and Strider would have to be monitored, I thought, as we wended our way back home. Their tendency to dash off madly could prove dangerous. It would be tragic if they were shot as suspected hunters in the King's forest.

A short distance from our house was a Swazi hut-cum-shack. It belonged to Grace, a large Swazi lady just a bit older than me. She made a living by washing and cleaning for some of the residents. I think she also brewed and sold beer, but I'm not sure. It was illegal. She was a warm, laughing woman and we used to chat in passing.

As I was returning home from a walk in the forest one evening at dusk, I realised that Arrow was missing. I ran back outside and called and whistled, 'Arrooww, ARRROW!'

There was no sign of her. What do I do now, I wondered? Dave wasn't home yet and darkness was setting in. I recalled glimpsing two guards in the forest. Had Arrow followed them?

Panicking now, I raced up to Grace's hut. 'Grace, I need to go to the King's house.'

'Now? Why is that?' she asked, looking puzzled.

'I think one of our dogs has followed the guards. Can you take me there? I won't find it in the dark, I've only been there once before.'

She shook her head doubtfully. 'There are snakes.'

I pleaded with her and eventually she agreed. We rushed back to our house and I closed the animals inside and grabbed a torch.

This was not the forest of the daytime, cool and restful. This was the forest of the night, black and eerie. Strange shapes loomed in the darkness as the torchlight skittered off branches and leaves and sharp claws plucked at our hair and clothing. We stumbled through undergrowth and between tree trunks for what seemed an eternity until at last we spotted a glimmer of light through the trees.

As we approached Grace held on to my arm and said softly, 'Wait.'

She called out in Siswati and three guards emerged on to the dimly lit veranda. She launched into a long monologue, pointing to me at intervals. When she finally fell silent, they shook their heads disinterestedly. She asked again. Looking bored, they turned and drifted back inside the house leaving us alone.

Disheartened and desperately worried, I followed Grace back through the forest. At long last we emerged at her hut and for a few moments I stood there, undecided about what to do next. As I gazed at the dark forest, something stirred in its depths. Something white.

'What's that?' I murmured, pointing.

Suddenly Arrow burst from amidst the trees, jumping up at me and barking joyously. Grace shook her head cynically. After this episode, I knew I would have to keep tabs on the dogs at all times.

Dave heard of a second-hand fridge for sale and we bought it. It was wonderful to have ice-blocks again. He met Brendan, an Irish vet who was employed at the state veterinary laboratory in Manzini. Brendan, his wife Mary and their two children Bevan and Sieff popped around to visit. When they discovered we had very little furniture, they lent us a few chairs and a dresser.

Once we had settled in, I planted a vegetable garden in the small area of open ground between the house and the forest. The soil was a bit sandy, but I decided to try anyway and planted lettuce, cabbage, onions, spinach and tomato seeds. I nurtured this garden, watering it religiously twice a day and before very long the seedlings popped up.

Early every morning, after Dave had set off for the clinic, I dressed in khaki shorts, a T-shirt and wellingtons and walked the veld, trailed by dogs and cats (but not Seafood – she still wasn't allowed).

Each direction brought new discoveries. A grove of guava trees laden with fruit, a gorge rampant with overhanging ferns, delicate water flowers in a stream. A marsh where you sank in up to your knees, and a rocky hillside scattered with huge prehistoric boulders covered in orange fungi and green and white lichen.

One morning, cresting a hill, we looked down on a large natural dam. The water was dark and I was wondering whether we could swim safely when the dogs began barking. Turning, I saw the guard I had met in the forest standing a short distance away. His face bore the look of someone who had just sucked bitter lemons.

'Morning,' I said.

He grunted sullenly.

'Pardon?'

'No fishing.'

'Fishing? What would I fish with? . . . See, no fishing rod.'

'NO FISHING . . . King's property' . . . he pointed to the dogs.

'They don't fish . . . they've never fished.'

He glared at me and stalked off.

We didn't swim that day but in the days that followed, after a long hot walk, we'd make a detour and stop at the dam for a swim. It was so hot that I would enter the water fully clothed and within ten minutes of emerging my clothes just steam-dried on me. The dogs would race into the water, splashing wildly and swimming in circles. Strangely, they never once caught a fish!

Most Sundays, Dave and I would rise before dawn. Followed by the dogs and cats we'd wend our way silently behind the neighbouring houses, along the outskirts of the forest. In the grove of guava trees we'd pause to pluck ripe fruit for breakfast. Then, pockets bulging, we'd climb a small hill covered in knee-high grass and indigenous shrubs. We'd often stumble across tortoises grazing peacefully on veld flowers. When they saw us they'd retreat into their shells with a *whoosh*, coming out only if we offered them pieces of guava.

Moving on, the path entered a shadowy wooded area bordered by a gorge. On one side the earth sloped steeply downwards, ending in a trickling stream at the bottom of the gorge. Following the path until we emerged into open grassland, we'd gaze down upon the dam in the hollow below.

This was usually the signal for the dogs to race ahead and plunge wildly into the cool murky water, while the cats rubbed quietly against our legs. No unseemly display of excitement for them.

Lying on the mossy grass at the water's edge, eating our guavas, we'd watch the sun come up over the horizon. When the first rays warmed the air around us, we'd enter the water, shivering at its cool silky touch. Later we'd amble slowly home, drinking in the smells and sounds of the bush.

One day as we arrived at the dam, I stopped abruptly and called the dogs to my side. Sunning itself on the water's edge was a huge leguaan, its prehistoric scales iridescent in the sunlight. With its thick, powerful tail it was at least two metres long. Its eyes flicked towards us and in one fluid movement it slid forward into the water with a faint *plop* and disappeared.

From that day on, we approached the dam cautiously, scanning the water and surrounding reeds carefully, before putting even our toes into it.

Snakes and Peacocks and Things

As the weeks passed we met the occupants of the other houses. In the house opposite ours lived a young South African couple and their son. They owned a beautiful black Labrador who got on well with our dogs. One day, a German couple who lived three houses down took Dave to one side and warned him that it was highly dangerous for me to walk the veld as I did, because of the abundance of snakes in the area.

'Yes,' I said, when he repeated this warning to me.

I was born to be wild, I had decided, and had absolutely no intention of curtailing the walks. When Africa calls, it calls LOUDLY.

Dave gave me a lecture on the symptoms caused by the bites of various species of snakes, in order that I would be able to recognise them if any of the animals were bitten. He told me the Siswati word for snake and made me repeat it several times. I was busy feeding the cats at the time and my concentration was somewhat lacking. By the next day I could not recall the word and only remembered that a certain type of snake venom caused nervous signs – twitching and jerking.

One morning I was sitting on the lounge floor sketching when Philby strolled in from outside. My heart did a somersault in my chest when I saw him. His left eye was hugely swollen, the white flesh inside his eyelid totally engorged and bulging outwards. I could not see his eyeball at all. Staring at him aghast, I wondered what to do. We were still waiting for the telephone to be connected and Dave had our only vehicle.

'*Why are you looking at me like that?*'

'Where is your eyeball?' I asked.

'*Oh . . . that. Don't worry about it,*' he shrugged carelessly.

'What do you mean, don't worry? What happened?'

'*Something spat in it.*'

'What kind of something?'

'*It looked like a thick rope, only shiny.*'

'My God, that's a snake!'

'*I was going to bring it home, but when it spat in my eye I left it.*'

'Are you mad?'

We sat on the floor facing each other. He gazed at me with one sparkling green eye as I watched anxiously for nervous symptoms.

'*You're still staring.*'

'I'm waiting for you to start twitching and jerking.'

'*Why? You're the one that's twitching.*'

Enough, I thought. Grabbing him by the scruff of the neck, I hauled him off to the kitchen and with my other hand I removed a bottle of milk from the fridge. Ripping the top off with my teeth, I poured milk lavishly over his eye. Unfortunately much of it gravitated into his ears. Amidst spluttering protests, I shut him in the spare room to await Dave's return.

Dave said it must have been a spitting cobra. Fortunately the swelling subsided after a day or two without any other side effects. It took a while longer to remove the dried milk from his ears.

We had been in Swaziland for five months when we began to suspect that I might be pregnant. Never having consulted a doctor in Manzini, we decided to have my urine sample tested at a pharmacy. Dave took it in and the pharmacist asked him to return in four days for the results.

'He gave me such a funny look,' Dave told me.

'What kind of look?'

'A sort of knowing look.'

'Why would he do that? It must be your imagination.'

Dave duly returned to the pharmacy for the results. As he entered, the pharmacist looked up at him with a commiserating face. He said, 'I'm afraid it's positive.'

'Oh wonderful!' blurted Dave and the two of them burst into laughter.

A few days later I heard a commotion outside – spitting, hissing and howling. It sounded like a cat fight and I ran to the door to investigate. There was not a cat in sight. The cacophony seemed to be coming from the veld above the ramp. I scrambled up the ramp on all fours and came face to face with Philby's backside. His frontside was challenging a huge Egyptian cobra. Reared up with hood inflated, it was swaying and hissing aggressively, only a metre away from Philby who crouched, ready to spring. At a glance I could see that this was a very cross snake.

There was only one thing I could do and so I did it. Reaching forward, I grabbed Philby's tail in a vice-grip and reversed down the ramp. At the bottom I seized him firmly by the scruff of the neck and marched him, kicking and screaming, to the spare room.

'It's MY SNAKE. I saw it FIRST.'

'*It's not your snake. It's wild.*'
'*I want it for my COLLECTION.*'
'*What collection?*'
'*MY SNAKE COLLECTION.*'
'There will be no snake collections ... NOT IN THIS HOUSE.'

Slamming the door and ignoring a shout of '*IT'S NOT FAIR!*', I picked up a spade and crawled back up the ramp. The snake, a gleaming golden colour, thick as my forearm, was still swaying and hissing furiously. Staring at it in fascination, I wished it would just go away quietly.

'Why don't you just go away quietly,' I murmured. It gave me a dirty look and hissed with renewed vigour.

Moving cautiously, I reached out with the spade and nudged it gently. As I did so, it hurled its body to the ground, uncoiling like lightning and gliding swiftly into the long grass. It was about three metres long and within seconds it had disappeared.

Much to his disgust, Philby was confined to the bedroom for the rest of the day. Just in case he decided to go out and find it again.

A few days later as I was washing the dishes, I glanced through the kitchen window up at the garden. It was on a higher level than the house and I could usually see the tops of my plants as they soaked up the sunlight. There was nothing there! Dropping the dish in the sink I raced out, only to stare in dismay at what was left of them. The tomato plants had been reduced to short little stubs with the odd leaf still adhering here and there. All that remained of the lettuces, which had been almost ready to pick, were a few wilted leaves lying on the ground. The spinach was gone, as were the cabbages.

What on earth could have done this, I wondered? I examined the ground but could find no trace of buck spoor, although in places the soil looked as if something had been dragged over it. I was unable to identify the marks. It was a complete mystery to me. There is something very satisfying about growing things, I reflected, but there is also something very satisfying about actually *eating* the things one has grown.

Later that morning the mystery was solved. I entered the lounge and was surprised to see all five cats huddled on the window sill peering up at the garden. Coming up behind them, I looked out to see a herd of peacocks sweeping through the grass towards the vegetable patch. They had come back for seconds.

Hurriedly I closed the outside door to keep the dogs and cats inside.

'*They're budgies,*' I heard Philby inform Carrots.

'*Oh really?*'

'*Yes, HUGE budgies . . . let's go get them.*' He patted his thigh to see if his dagger was still strapped to it.

'You are not going anywhere,' I stated firmly.

By this time the dogs had noticed the peacocks too and Arrow and Strider were raring to go. The house was reduced to chaos, with the dogs barking excitedly and Philby shrieking defiantly, '*Leave the poor little plants alone!*'

I slipped through the door, closed it behind me and walked up into the garden. As I stood there gazing at the devastation, my friend the royal guard emerged from the forest wearing his usual dour expression.

'King's peacocks,' he muttered.

'Pardon?'

'KING'S PEACOCKS!'

'Oh.'

'No hunt King's peacocks!'

'No . . . of course not.'

'Dave?'

'Hmmm.'

'We're going to have to move.'

'Why?'

'The Royal Peacocks . . . they're not going to live long.'

'Hmmm.'

Running the clinic from the mobile home in Manzini was not working out. It was very hot inside and there were no facilities for hospitalising animals overnight. This was a problem, as some animals needed to be in hospital.

We had heard of a house on a smallholding that might be suitable as a combined home and clinic. The previous tenants had returned overseas and, after obtaining permission from the owner, we set off to view it.

The entrance to the property was on the opposite side of the Manzini road from where we were presently living. Instead of turning right on to the dirt track leading to our house, we turned left on to a larger dirt road. The road continued parallel to the highway for a short distance before curving inland. At the curve we veered left on to a bumpy dirt and grass track, coming to a halt at a double gate. We opened the gate and drove into a large parking area. The house lay to the right. Facing us were several outbuildings and a garage, and on the highway side there was an old wooden stable and a long trellis covered in vines.

The owner had given us a set of keys for all the various buildings. From the large sitting-room windows we gazed down into a valley and beyond it to the hills which unfolded one after another like smooth meringue. Those closest to us were a soft green, but as they retreated into the distance they became draped in a blue and purple haze.

In the garden we discovered a swimming-pool surrounded by mossy lawn, brightly blooming hibiscus bushes and a weeping willow tree. The willow made me think of Penny and Russell . . . and, less fondly, of the rooster.

To us, the house and its surroundings seemed like paradise on earth. As far as the veterinary side was concerned, the storeroom could be converted into a consulting room-cum-theatre. With all the additional buildings we could easily hospitalise animals, or we could even use one of the bedrooms for this purpose. The house had three and we only needed one.

Deciding then and there to take it, we gave one month's notice at the prefab house.

The month slipped by and suddenly it was our last day. We would be moving the following day, a Sunday. Around mid-morning, as I was busy cleaning and packing, I smelt bush burning. I went outside to investigate and realised that the air was hazy with smoke. Feeling slightly uneasy, I crossed the dirt track, walked past the house opposite ours and climbed a mound for a better view. My blood ran cold at the sight before me.

A long wall of flame, less than half a kilometre away, was advancing rapidly in my direction. Running ahead of the flames were buck, at least twenty of them. I stood mesmerised for a moment and then I turned and ran to the house opposite ours.

'Corné!' I shouted. 'BUSHFIRE!'

She came out looking bewildered.

'Quickly . . . get your son and your dog into the car and move it across to our house.' She stared at me doubtfully.

'*Do it!*' I cried. 'That fire is moving.'

Leaving her, I ran back to our house and began closing dogs and cats inside. Every one of them was there, except Philby. Typical.

I quickly dialled Dave's number and told him urgently, 'Dave, you must come home *now* . . . a bushfire is heading this way.'

'I'm on my way.'

I ran outside to look for Philby. The fire was much closer now, the flames visible from our driveway. I called desperately, 'PHILBY . . . Philbeee!' There was no sign of him.

Corné had put her young son and their dog in the car which was still parked next to their house.

'Get that car out of here!' I shouted.

My concern was a valid one. Thick veld extended right up to a clump of bluegums growing against their garden fence. The houses below theirs were semi-protected by a fairly deep gorge, which would act as a firebreak.

Ash was already floating down around us, as Corné moved the car across to our house. Connecting her garden hosepipe, I began wetting the house and the bush against the fence. Suddenly the fire was upon us. Buck jack-knifed through the bush, some bounding past us, others into the gorge. Our bakkie came down the track. Thank God, I thought.

Corné screamed and pointed. The leaves high up in the bluegums were alight and the trees began burning fiercely. Dave appeared at my side, taking the hosepipe from me. The smoke was now so thick that I was gasping for breath. Somehow the small stream of water was having an effect on the burning bluegums.

Then the fire jumped the gorge and the bush growing against the houses below ignited into flames. A large fire engine came down the track, coming to a halt just below us. Fire-fighters jumped down and began unrolling a huge fire-hose.

'Look at that!' Dave shouted, pointing at something.

Following the direction of his finger, I saw Philby stroll calmly from the burning gorge. Slinking in under the fire engine, he watched the firemen, enthralled.

Before he realised what was happening, I had him firmly by the scruff of his neck. Protesting loudly, he was hauled back to the house and shut in the spare room.

'*I just wanted to watch their snake,*' he murmured sadly. His whiskers were short charcoal stubs on his face.

'That was NOT a snake. That was a fire-hose.'

'*Oh.*'

We fought the fire all afternoon. By late afternoon it had died down and appeared to be under control. The main problem was water. Our water came from a natural dam on top of the hill and was piped to the houses by PVC piping laid across the veld. At one stage there was a break in the piping and this had to be found and repaired with the fire still raging.

At dusk the wind came up and the fire broke out again. This time it came sweeping through the veld from the top road, heading towards the forest.

Throughout the night the men in our small community and the royal guards fought the blaze in a desperate effort to prevent it from reaching the forest. By dawn they had managed to extinguish it. The water in the dam was very low and opening a tap in the house provided only a trickle of water. There was no question of a bath.

Later that morning we packed our possessions and, blackened and stinking, we moved over the highway into the new house.

If the Cat Fits . . .

'I'm on my way to check a horse on Mrs Pocock's farm,' Dave said, entering the kitchen. 'Why don't you come with me? I'd like you to meet her.'

'All right.'

Mrs Pocock and I had never met, but I knew she was one of Dave's favourite clients.

We stepped through the farmhouse door into a small lobby. The lobby contained a very large washing machine, on top of which lay a very large white goat. It was fast asleep. And snoring.

After a moment's hesitation, I decided not to comment, but Mrs Pocock, noticing the direction of my gaze said, 'Oh, this is Nanny. The washing machine is her favourite resting place.'

I noticed with relief that the washing machine was not switched on, my mind boggling at the thought of a large goat vibrating gently as it went through its cycles.

'Actually, Doctor, I'm looking for a home for her. Would you be interested?'

Dave's face lit up but before he could say 'Yes' I gave him a very meaningful look. Closing his mouth on the yes, he said that he and I would have to discuss it.

On the way home I waited for him to broach the subject.

I didn't have long to wait.

'Love, goat's milk is very healthy. Especially for you now that you're pregnant,' he said deviously.

'Dave, we can't possibly take the goat.'

'But why not? We could make our own cheese.'

A picture flashed into my mind. Of myself in an advanced stage of pregnancy, squatting on the ground, forehead resting on the goat's flank as I tried to milk it.

'I'm sorry, but we can't,' I said firmly.

'Well, why not?'

'We don't have a washing machine.'

'Now you're being ridiculous. It doesn't have to sleep on a washing machine.'

'Where would it sleep then?'

'It can sleep on any raised hard surface.'

'Dave, the only raised hard surfaces we have are the kitchen sink and the dresser that Brendan loaned us.'

'It can sleep on the dresser then.'

'No, it can't. Brendan wouldn't like it.'

Very reluctantly, Dave abandoned the idea of taking the goat, fortunately without following up the kitchen sink option. In my opinion, the writing was on the wall – and for once it was in English.

Nanny would've started off sleeping on the dresser and before long she would be lolling on the couch with us, watching TV. With her legs crossed, eating popcorn.

A week after we moved into the new house Dave went out and bought a second-hand lounge suite. It consisted of a three-seater couch and a two-seater couch upholstered in lime-green and cream material. The material was a bit soiled and I decided to wash the whole suite with foam carpet cleaner. Brushing off the surface dust and dirt first, I pushed the brush into the deep groove between the backrest and

the seat. There was a *clunk* as it hit something hard. I reached in and pulled the object out.

It was a vicious-looking curved dagger. Staring at it in astonishment, I wondered how on earth it had come to be there. Had the couch been involved in a murder? Were teams of international policemen still hunting desperately for the murder weapon? I examined the blade closely and was relieved to find no trace of bloodstains. I spent the rest of the day speculating on its history.

Exploring the garden at the new house was like going on an expedition into new territory. The property was so large that each day we discovered something new.

One morning Whippy brought me an avocado pear. Taking it from her mouth, I saw that it was ripe.

'I hope you didn't steal this?'

'*No, I found it.*'

'In someone's basket, I suppose,' I remarked cynically. Where food was concerned her thieving activities still knew no boundaries.

'*It was on the ground,*' she said with a reproachful look. '*Come, I'll show you.*'

She led me to a far corner of the smallholding where two huge avocado trees stood. They were laden with fruit. The ground beneath them was littered with gleaming avos. Whippy placed her paw on one and began tearing off the peel with her teeth, before eating the soft creamy inside.

This was splendid! Dave and I ate them for breakfast, lunch and supper. We had avo salad, stuffed avo, avo on toast, until we were heartily sick of them.

In the fertile black soil of the vegetable garden I found a well-established strawberry patch. Every few days it yielded a handful of juicy red strawberries, sweeter than any I'd ever tasted before. At the corner of the vegetable garden stood a huge bauhinia tree covered in a mantle of translucent, delicately scented pink flowers.

We were still in the process of settling in when Creepy slunk into our lives. I went into the sitting-room one lunchtime and found Dave sitting on the couch with a thin scabby dog at his feet. When it saw me, it promptly urinated on the floor, before hiding behind Dave's legs.

'And this?' I asked, indicating the dog who was cowering wetly on the floor.

'He belongs to a client. He has bad mange. The dog, not the client.'

'I can see that,' I murmured. The dog was pathetic, its coat almost non-existent, its skin covered in festering sores.

'I'm keeping him here until the infected skin has cleared up. Once the infection has cleared the owner can carry on with the mange treatment.'

'Dave, must he be in the house with us?' The smell was quite bad.

'Well, he's so timid. I thought we could socialise him a bit.'

'What's his name?'

'He doesn't have a name.'

'I'll call him Creepy.'

And so, temporarily, Creepy moved in with us. Over the first few days he cringed and urinated nervously each time we spoke to him. Reaching out to touch him elicited the same reaction and I had some interesting thoughts about his owner. Dave pointed out that the man, a bank clerk, was concerned enough to bring him for treatment.

'Hmmm,' I replied.

After two weeks of treatment and gentle handling, Creepy's fear gradually subsided and his skin improved daily. As his confidence grew, he began to behave like a normal, well-adjusted dog, coming to us for attention with his tail wagging.

Brendan and Mary had become close friends and called to visit us every now and again. Mary began putting pressure on me to see a doctor. We estimated that I was approximately three months pregnant and it was time to see a doctor.

'More than time,' Mary said.

She arranged for me to see an American missionary doctor based at Manzini hospital.

Dr Armstrong was tall and thin, with a look of dedication. After the examination, he said everything appeared to be normal and suggested that I see him once a month for a check-up.

When we first moved into our new home, the water in the swimming pool was a dark green colour, thick and murky.

'If crocodiles were breeding in there we wouldn't be any the wiser,' I remarked to Dave.

It took him a while to repair the pump and treat the water, which gradually changed to a clear blue.

One hot Sunday morning he pronounced the pool ready. There was a general stampede in its direction and I managed to dive in first, closely followed by Mandy, Whippy, Arrow and Strider. Sally had to be lifted in. We wallowed in the sparkling water, luxuriating in its coolness. Philby, Carrots and Nuggie hung around at the water's edge and after a while I lifted first one and then another into the water. They seemed to enjoy it.

I noticed Splittie watching us but when I moved towards her she gave me a look that said, '*Touch me and you die.*'

Later that morning there was a knock on the kitchen door

and I opened it to find a middle-aged couple on the veranda. The woman was cradling a grey and white striped cat in her arms. They were Italian and it soon became apparent that we could not understand each other. They spoke no English and I speak no Italian. I hurried to fetch Dave (who doesn't speak Italian either).

When Dave arrived on the scene the man pointed to the cat and said repeatedly, 'ALFIE . . . ALFIE.'

Dave and I nodded. The cat's name was Alfie. Dave pointed to the cat and said, 'ALFIE'. They nodded and we nodded. More sign language followed. Pointing his index finger downwards the man moved it in circles and then mimed lifting a stylus on to a record.

It took me a few seconds to grasp what he was doing. I was absolutely mystified. What did music have to do with the cat? Dave nodded again.

Then the man launched into a series of spastic movements, hunching his shoulders and jerking his arms which he held outstretched in front of him. Staring at him open-mouthed it suddenly dawned upon me. Now I had it! This cat liked dancing.

Smiling at the cat admiringly, I turned to Dave. 'He's saying the cat likes dancing.'

'No he's not.'

'What is he saying then?'

'He's saying the cat is an epileptic and had a fit behind their record player.'

'Oh.'

Slightly embarrassed, I left, pretending to be busy elsewhere. When I returned the couple were driving off in their van. Dave, holding Alfie in his arms, was watching as the van disappeared through the gate.

'Oh!' I said, surprised. 'They've left him here.'

'Mmmm,' Dave murmured.

'When are they coming back for him?'

'I'm not sure if they are.'

'What do you mean?'

'I think they've given him to us.'

All Dave had been able to establish was that the couple were moving to Piggs Peak. When he enquired as to when they would be returning, they nodded enthusiastically, patted Alfie on the head, climbed into their van and drove off. We were not sure whether or not we had just acquired another cat.

Alfie was a male. He was short-haired and wore an air of vulnerability, as if he had been battered by life. A humble cat, he accepted his change of circumstances without question. His not to reason why.

Two days later as I was sitting on the couch reading, I noticed that he was acting strangely. He was standing staring fixedly into space with his tail, stiff as a board, sticking out horizontally behind him. After maintaining this stance for about fifteen minutes, he suddenly keeled over on to his side with a thud. His legs began kicking sporadically as saliva foamed from his mouth and a pool of urine formed on the floor.

'Dave, come quickly!' I shouted. I bent down next to Alfie, speaking soothingly and stroking his fur. By the time Dave arrived he had stopped convulsing but seemed exhausted and confused.

Dave went to fetch some epileptic medication from the surgery. He said that in the beginning it would be a case of trial and error as to what dosage to give him, and how often, because we didn't know the frequency of his fits.

After a while I offered him a saucer of milk which he drank gratefully before lapsing into a deep sleep.

The other cats, with the exception of Seafood, accepted Alfie's presence quite calmly. Almost as if they knew he was different, they never challenged his right to be there. Splittie, of course, ignored him because he was Italian.

'*I don't mix with foreigners,*' she sneered. '*They have strange habits.*'

Seafood, on the other hand, was terrified of him. She had been present when he had his first fit and had run screaming from the room. I blamed this on Splittie's over-protectiveness. She was the ultimate domineering mother and Seafood's personality was being repressed.

'You never allow her to do anything on her own,' I told Splittie.

'*I'm protecting her. I'm her mother.*'

'Protecting her from what?'

'*Well, FROM HER for one,*' she gestured towards Whippy, who quickly averted her eyes.

'Whippy only wants to love her.'

'*Huh,*' she said nastily, cuffing Seafood behind the head before stalking out the room. Seafood followed her meekly.

When I returned from the supermarket one Saturday morning, I discovered that Creepy had been discharged. I was disappointed at not being able to say goodbye. Over the weeks he had changed so much from the pathetic little dog we had first seen. His skin had healed, the scabs were gone and hair was growing nicely where there had been bare patches before. But the change that most warmed my heart was the fact that he had become a happy dog, eyes bright and tail wagging as he came to greet you.

'I hope he's going to be all right.'

'He'll be fine,' Dave said. 'The owner only has to bath him for another couple of weeks. The mange is 90 per cent cured.

Creepy, living up to his name, had crept into my heart.

Passing the Buck

My khaki shorts were feeling a bit tight. It was clearly time to invest in some maternity dresses. Manzini was not exactly the shopping Mecca of Africa and I walked the town flat to find something suitable. In the end I managed to find two dresses. They weren't maternity dresses but they were loose-fitting and would have to do.

By now I was due for a second check-up at the hospital and as Dr Armstrong palpated my abdomen, he glanced at my side. 'What happened here, did you fall?'

To my surprise I saw two large purple bruises, one on my hip and the other on my thigh. I stared down at the bruises. I couldn't recall bumping into anything.

'I haven't fallen,' I said. 'I don't know how they got there.'

I told him I had developed evening sickness and was finding it difficult to sleep at night. I tried to describe how tired I was, but he said this was normal in pregnancy and was most probably exacerbated by the extreme Swaziland heat. Dave had said the same thing. Frustrated at not being fully understood, I kept quiet. Sometimes when I woke in the mornings, I felt as if there was a plughole under one of my feet and that all my energy had leaked out during the night.

When Dave was still working from the mobile home, he had employed a Swazi woman called Esther to assist him. She was a wonderful person, warm-hearted and kind. And very efficient. When we moved to the new house she travelled back and forth every day by bus.

Gradually, as the pregnancy sapped my energy, she started helping me in the house with washing and cleaning and Dave decided to employ a second assistant, someone who would live on the premises, help in the garden and go on farm calls with him. And so Joseph Dlamini entered our lives. He was young, only seventeen, and a bit wary of us at first. After all, we were white South Africans. But this reticence soon passed and a mutual liking grew between us.

Strider and Arrow had become very difficult to keep tabs on. The property was so big that sometimes I had no idea where they were. Joseph brought me a message from my friend, the royal guard. He said he had seen the two dogs wandering unaccompanied in the forest. Since the fire he had mellowed and become quite friendly. We appreciated his concern and began closing the two dogs in the changing room when we were busy. It had a metal fretwork door and was ideal for this purpose.

Occasionally Whippy and I would cross the highway and walk in the forest. Here the perpetual twilight was broken only by dapples of sunlight filtering through from above. Ambling along slowly and breathing in the rich loamy smell of decaying vegetation, we would enjoy the cool silence, disturbed now and then by the call of a bird or the high-pitched buzz of cicadas. More than any church service, the peaceful beauty of God's creation renewed my spirit.

But most days around sunset, Dave and I and the animals would walk a trail that wound along the borders of the smallholding. When we were past the avocado trees we entered an area of waist-high grass interspersed with tumbles of rocks that made me think of ancient burial sites.

The grass gave way to shoulder-height bush and taller trees as, gradually, the path slid downhill into the valley. Here, apart from the odd clearing strewn with brilliantly coloured veld flowers, the bush was thick and impenetrable. Sometimes we would sit under a thorn tree and just listen to the sounds of the veld. Then the path climbed up again into thick grass and tall reeds, ending near the house.

To an observer, we must have resembled a group going on safari. Walking in single file along the narrow path, there was a definite pecking order.

Mandy took the lead, checking the path for any sign of danger, with Dave immediately behind her. Close on his heels came Strider and Arrow. Too close on his heels actually. They were always trying to push past him and run off wildly into the bush. They were a bit of a handful, those two. Philby was next, calling out to any leopard that might be listening: '*Come and get me . . . I'm ready for you.*' Whippy would be in the middle, then Splittie and Seafood and myself.

I can still picture Splittie's pugnacious little backside on the path before me. Stomping along officiously, every now and again her paw would flash out and cuff Seafood on the head. *Control* was a concept Splittie believed in.

Trailing along behind me would be a ragtag group consisting of Alfie, Carrots, Nuggie and sometimes Sally, if she felt up to it. She was feeling her age now, and her hind legs had a tendency to give way.

One evening a large buck broke from a thicket just ahead

of us. Dave was desperately trying to restrain the dogs, when I thought I saw Whippy's tan body bounding through the bush after it. Terrified that she would be gored, I gave chase. Shouting, 'WHIPPY . . . WHIPPPEEE!' I stumbled after her, thorn trees and branches tearing at my clothes. Why was she not responding? She was usually so obedient. Each time I got close, she would bound away deeper into the bush. Then I heard a faint cry from Dave in the valley: 'Chrystal, it's OK. Whippy's here with me.'

I had been chasing the buck.

Scratched and bleeding, I staggered back to the group.

'You know, Dave . . . I think I almost caught it,' I said.

He just looked at me expressionlessly.

The storms in Swaziland were unlike any I had ever experienced before. Bolts of lightning were hurled furiously earthwards, as if someone up there was in a rage. Cataclysmic rolls of thunder caused the house to shudder and water burst from the clouds as if squeezed by a giant hand. If one was caught outside in the rain, one felt as if the drops were piercing one's skin.

One night at bedtime we heard the dull rumble of a storm in the distance. The animals were restless and so we took them all into the bedroom with us. Lying in the dark, we watched as lightning struck the distant hills.

After a while I said, 'Dave?'

'Yes?'

'That lightning is heading this way.'

'Hmmm.'

As we watched, the lightning struck closer and closer, like an ancient warrior marching across the hills towards our bedroom window. Jagged streaks of vertical light shot from the heavens straight into the ground, followed by explosions of thunder. We began counting the seconds between lightning and thunder. The intervals became shorter and shorter. One . . . two . . . three . . . four . . . five. One . . . two . . . three . . . four. One . . . two.

We jumped in fear as it struck in the valley below the property and the air was rent by a tremendous crack of thunder. Hearts thudding, we held our breath, waiting for the next bolt.

Suddenly, shockingly, it was there. A brilliant shaft of light streaked from the sky hitting the tree outside our window. Blinded by the flash, we cringed as thunder crashed in the room with us. The dogs yelped. The cats tried to hide, terrified. And then it was gone.

We lay in silence. After a few minutes, Dave picked up a torch and I followed him outside to look at the tree. It was scorched black. Still warm to the touch, the charcoal bark crumbled in our hands.

When we had first moved into the house we had decided not to have a second telephone installed in the surgery. Not only was it expensive but there was a long waiting period involved. Our only telephone was in the sitting-room, and as a result I spent a good part of my day answering calls for the surgery.

We are all victims of Pavlov's experiments with those dogs, I thought one morning as I rushed out to call Dave for the fourth time that day. The almost invariable routine was that I would have to rush out to call him and, if he was busy, rush back and find out what the caller wanted, and then out again to consult Dave, and then back again with the answer. It was driving me mad.

Still, despite this, when the telephone rang at 8.30 one evening, I hurried down the passage to answer it. With a baby monkey perched on top of my head.

It was my mother. 'Hello my child, how are you?'

'Fine, thanks.'

As we exchanged news, the monkey clambered down my arm and leapt for the telephone cord. Grasping it with both hands, it began swinging gently. Back and forth, back and forth, a tiny Tarzan of the Jungle, only hairier.

After a while its swinging became more enthusiastic and the phone began to crackle.

'Chrystal, there's interference on this line, should I try again later?'

'It isn't interference, it's a monkey.'

There was a deep silence on the other end.

'What monkey?'

'There's a baby monkey swinging on the cord, making the phone crackle.'

'Why is it swinging on the cord?'

'I suppose it likes to. It was sitting on my head when I answered the phone.'

'You shouldn't be handling monkeys while you're pregnant.'

'Why not?'

'You know what they say. Your baby will be born looking like a monkey.'

'Who are *they*?' I asked.

Typically, my mother managed to end the conversation without identifying 'they'. When she didn't want to answer a question, she just ignored it and changed the subject. This was done quite blatantly. There was no subtlety involved.

For years I had been trying to establish who 'they' were, without any success. I strongly suspected that my mother herself was the origin of these old wives' tales.

During my childhood I had often heard her say sharply to my Dad when we were out driving: 'John, *slow down*. You're driving like the Hobs of Hell.'

When I asked who these people were, she said it didn't matter. I was about eighteen years old before I discovered that the Hobsovell were not an Irish family living down the road. With a father who drove like a maniac.

Shaking my head, I replaced the receiver but before I could remove the monkey, the phone rang again. This time it was one of Dave's clients and I could hear she was in quite a state.

'Is your husband there?'

'Yes, he's around somewhere.'

'It's Mrs Baines speaking, from Big Bend. Please call him to the phone. We have a suspected rabies case here.'

Hastily, I went to find Dave. 'Rabies' is a word that rings alarm bells in anyone's mind.

While he was speaking to Mrs Baines I detached the monkey from the cord and carried it into our bedroom to give it its bottle. Lying contentedly on its back in a cardboard box, swathed in a soft blanket, it sucked happily. Its parents had been shot by a farmer and we were trying to find a home for it. With the approaching birth of our own baby, we could not keep it ourselves. Even if my mother's gloomy predictions came true and they were the spitting image of each other. We both knew that taking on a monkey is a tricky business. As they grow older, problems such as biting and possessiveness arise.

Whippy, of course, wanted to keep the monkey for herself. *'Can't I keep it?'*

'No, I'm sorry.'

'It's so sweet,' she said, gazing at it wistfully.

'I know, but soon you'll have all the baby you can handle.'

'Will it look like this one?'

'Hopefully not.'

Splittie, on the other hand, wanted nothing to do with it. When we introduced its box into our bedroom, she packed her things and moved out to the sitting-room.

'And I won't be back until it's gone,' she tossed over her shoulder as she stalked from the room in high dudgeon.

'Don't be silly, it's only a baby,' I called after her.

'Dirty, smelly little thing.'

'Really Splittie, that's unfair.'

'And don't you dare touch it,' she hissed at Seafood. *'You'll pick up some nasty disease.'*

When I returned to the sitting-room, Dave was still on the phone, this time to Brendan.

'Fine, Brendan. Ten o'clock. Thanks.'

'What was all that about?' I asked as he replaced the receiver.

'I'll tell you in a minute,' he said, dialling again.

'Hello, Mrs Baines? Will you bring Wheels in at 10 o'clock tomorrow? One of the state vets will meet us here and he suggests that your son accompany you. I'll see you tomorrow then. Goodbye.'

Looking worried, Dave told me that the Baines' dog Wheels had suddenly started acting strangely. Within a day, he had changed from a happy-go-lucky dog into an extremely aggressive one and had bitten their ten-year-old son Gary. Dave had seen Wheels the week before for his vaccination and he had seemed perfectly normal then. It was already late in the day and so the Baines family had decided to bring him in the next morning, rather than drive all the way from Big Bend at night. In the meantime Brendan was trying to organise antirabies inoculation for Gary.

The next morning Dave came to call me when Mrs Baines and Gary arrived. He was bringing them in to wait in the house while he and Brendan examined Wheels.

'He's foaming at the mouth and trying to bite the cage bars and it's upsetting for them. Make them some tea, will you? They're very tense, especially young Gary.'

I put the kettle on as Dave ushered them in. They looked rather white around the gills, I noticed. Over a cup of tea, they gradually unwound. Whippy was making friends with Gary and the cats were lying around in various stages of relaxation. The peaceful sound of birdsong drifted through the open French windows.

I was chatting happily when I noticed Mrs Baines suddenly staring at the floor with a rigid face. Glancing down, I saw that Alfie had fallen over on to the rug and was twitching and jerking, prior to full convulsions. As one, the Baines family sprang to their feet, ready to flee.

Quickly crouching down next to Alfie, I said reassuringly, 'Don't worry, he's epileptic, he's having a fit.'

Just at that moment, as Alfie's convulsions reached their pitch, Brendan strode in.

'Hello, hello . . . what's this? Another one?' he asked cheerfully. He knew perfectly well that Alfie was epileptic. I gave him one of my looks. Really, these animals made normal social interaction very difficult at times.

Picking Alfie up, I carried him through to our bedroom and laid him on the bed. He seemed so vulnerable after a fit, eyes unfocused and confused, as if he didn't understand what was happening to him. After giving him his tablet, I returned to the sitting-room.

Dave and Brendan were discussing the situation with

Mrs Baines.

'We've decided to hospitalise Wheels in a cage at the State Vet Laboratory,' Brendan was saying. 'We won't handle him for the next ten days but we'll see that he has food and water.'

Once an animal shows symptoms of rabies it dies within ten days. If Wheels lived for more than ten days, we would know he did not have rabies. The only other alternative was to euthanase him and send his brain away to be tested. He was the Baines' beloved family dog and they did not want him euthanased if it wasn't necessary. His symptoms were fairly typical though: fear of water, fear of light, extreme aggression and foaming at the mouth.

Brendan had contacted the hospital in Mbabane who confirmed that they had the antirabies inoculation for Gary. They left for the hospital, where Gary would have the first in a series of injections.

The morning had been rather stressful in one way or another, I thought as I wandered outside. Dave was back in the surgery, busy with another client. I strolled over to the grapevine to look for a bunch of grapes. All the grapes on one side of the trellis had been eaten, but there were plenty on the other side. Making my way around the garage and along the fence to a place where it sagged, I climbed over into the waist-high grass, and then walked back to the vine where clusters of dusky purple grapes hung in profusion. I picked one and popped it into my mouth. It was delicious, sweet and juicy, and as I ate another, and another, I felt the morning's stress drifting away.

Suddenly Joseph appeared on the other side of the trellis and stared at me through the vine.

'Morning, Ma'am.'

'Morning, Joseph.'

'Ma'am, I saw a speeeting cobra.'

'Oh,' I said, only mildly interested, and slightly irritated by the human intrusion.

'It was BEEG, Ma'am,' he said, holding one hand high over his head to indicate its length.

Popping a grape into my mouth, I asked casually, 'When did you see the snake, Joseph?'

'Five minutes ago, Ma'am.'

'Oh,' I said, plucking off another grape. 'Where did you see it?'

'There where you are standing, Ma'am.'

I froze with a grape halfway to my mouth and stared at Joseph through the trellis. Then my eyes moved. They flicked to the right. No snake. Then to the left. No snake. Should I look behind me? I hesitated. What if I turned around and looked into the smiling eyes of a spitting cobra? Then again, what if I did *not* turn around and there was, in fact, a spitting cobra about to sink its teeth into the back of my head. It was a dilemma.

Slowly, without moving my feet, I swivelled the top half of my body and looked behind me. Nothing. Then to the other side. Nothing. Standing very still, I ran my eyes over the vine. A snake could easily melt into the background of the twisted brown stems. It occurred to me that the quickest way out of my predicament would be to climb over the trellis. But I was pregnant and it was high, about two metres. A second option was to run madly through the tall thick grass shouting 'AIYEEEeeeee!' – an act guaranteed to antagonise any self-respecting snake.

Forcing myself to remain calm, I assessed the distance to the spot where the fence sagged on my left, and to the end of the stables on my right. It was approximately 20 metres either way. The grass was equally long and thick in both directions, but somehow the way past the back of the stables seemed marginally shorter. Taking a deep breath I set out, one careful step at a time. Fear crouched on my shoulder, whispering in my ear with each step, and my eyes scanned the grass like a roving camera. A few metres from the corner of the stables, unable to stand it any longer, I burst into a trot. Rounding the corner, I collided with Joseph. He had been watching my progress, spade in hand. Collapsing against the wooden wall, I exhaled slowly.

As I tottered back to the house, Dave called out from the surgery, 'Chrystal, come and look at this.'

'Not now,' I called back in an unnaturally high voice.

Strangely, when confronted by snakes on previous occasions I had never felt the fear I experienced on that day. In a face-to-face confrontation we could see each other and either of us, or both, could simply back off. When you know a snake is near and you cannot see it, the situation becomes dangerous. You may inadvertently step on it, or disturb it, and get bitten.

On the seventh day after Wheels was hospitalised at the State Laboratory, he started eating and drinking. Up until then he had touched nothing. This was good news and Brendan started him on a course of antibiotics mixed into his food.

Although he was beginning to react normally, he still seemed a bit off-balance. When ten days had passed we were sure he wasn't rabid but, even so, Brendan did not want to take any chances and kept him for another four days. On the fourteenth day, Dave went to fetch him. Mrs Baines had arranged to collect him from us the next day.

Dave and Brendan diagnosed an atypical reaction to the vaccination, causing a meningitis. Neither had seen such a case before.

When Dave brought Wheels home, he ran excitedly in circles. Smaller circles and bigger circles, but always circles. He was very pleased to see us, but the meningitis had caused damage to the brain and he could no longer move in a straight line. We hoped that this would improve with time. As I watched him, it occurred to me that his wheels just needed a bit of adjusting.

We found a home for the baby monkey with a man who had another that he was fostering. At least he would be able to socialise with his own kind. Sadly, I watched the man leave with the monkey. It was in the nick of time, as I was becoming too attached to it.

Like a waking cat, my maternal instincts had been roused from a deep slumber. Stretching and yawning, they were gazing about them with interest.

A Bleeding Shame

As I walked past Splittie in the long passage running from the sitting-room to our bedroom she lashed out playfully, her claws raking my ankle.

'Ow,' I exclaimed, dabbing at the welling blood with a tissue.

But I was busy with housework and bustled on with my chores. Half an hour later I noticed my right foot felt wet and sticky. Removing my shoe, I found it awash with blood. I wiped the blood from the scratch and watched as it welled up again and trickled down on to the floor. Strange, I thought, it's only a surface scratch. Why is it still bleeding? I sat down on the bed and applied pressure to the scratch and eventually, after about ten minutes, the bleeding stopped. I wondered uneasily whether I had developed some dread disease.

Alfie's fits now appeared to be under control. I watched him constantly for signs of an aura and if I saw him staring into space with a rigid tail, I would immediately dose him and avert the fit.

I was lying in bed late one night with the lights off when

I heard a thumping sound coming from the sitting-room. After a few seconds I realised that it must be Alfie having a fit. As I hurried down the passage in the dark I almost collided with Seafood who was running madly in the opposite direction. Alfie was definitely having a fit.

I found him kicking and jerking on the sitting-room floor. His feet were pedalling rhythmically against the door, causing the sound which had alerted me. I picked him up and carried him, still convulsing, to the spare room at the end of the passage. It was filled with boxes, some empty, others yet to be unpacked. Clearing a space on the floor I laid him down, closed the door, and went to fetch his medication. I popped the tablet down his throat and crouched next to him, stroking him.

As my eyes became accustomed to the gloom, I spotted Seafood huddled in a corner, illuminated by the moonlight. Oh no! I had closed her in the room with Alfie, the object of her terror.

'Oh Seafood, I'm so sorry, I didn't know you were in here,' I whispered, moving towards her. She shot past me through the open door and down the passage. I went after her, wanting to stop her and calm her down.

As she drew level with the kitchen door, Philby emerged. Head thrown back, mouth open, all four of his legs were jerking violently as though he was in the throes of a seizure. Seafood froze. Then her feet seemed to recover and in a wheelspin of naked terror she hurtled through the open French windows and into the garden. There was no chance of finding her now.

Worriedly, I turned to help Philby. He was sitting serenely on the floor, one front paw curled up before him as he nonchalantly examined his claws. For a moment we stared at each other. Then his eyes shifted away and he pretended to be interested in a moth on the wall.

'PHILBY!'

'What?'

'How could you?'

'What?'

'You deliberately pretended to have a fit. To frighten Seafood.'

'I wasn't trying to frighten her. I was practising.'

'Practising for what?'

'For the stage.'

'The stage!' I hissed. 'Well, let me tell you, if we don't find her . . . you'll tread the boards all right.'

As I walked back down the passage to the bedroom, I heard Philby mutter darkly to Carrots that *'even Laurence Olivier wouldn't get anywhere in this house'*.

Late the next morning Seafood crept back into the house. It took days of pampering to repair her shattered nerves.

My bouts of evening sickness were getting worse. After a particularly violent bout of vomiting, I noticed that small veins had burst in my eyes. The whites of my eyes now had patches of red blood in them. I wondered if there were any local productions of Dracula I could audition for. A few days later, small veins below my eyes also ruptured. I was worried, but too tired to make the effort to see Dr Armstrong.

One Sunday, I went looking for Dave to tell him that lunch was ready. As I entered the consulting room I saw that he was busy with a dog on the table. Two smartly dressed Swazi men were standing at the table, holding the dog.

Dave turned to me. 'Chrystal, go back to the house, I'll be there shortly. I'm busy with a euthanasia.'

Nodding, I turned to go and then stopped. There was something familiar about the dog. I turned back and stared, unsure. It looked like Creepy, but even Creepy had never looked as bad as this.

This dog was skin and bone. It was cringing on the table, its hairless skin a mass of huge suppurating sores.

'Dave, is it Creepy?' He nodded grimly. Approaching the table, I looked into Creepy's dull, defeated eyes. Devoid of hope, he gazed back at me as I stroked his head. The anger boiled up from my toes, erupting as I confronted his owner.

'How could you allow him to get into this state?'

Dave tried to stop me but I could not contain myself. 'Couldn't you follow simple instructions . . . *just look at him!*'

'Chrystal, please go back to the house.'

'You shouldn't be allowed to have a dog!' I shouted. 'This is criminal!' Then I burst into tears and stormed out.

Ten minutes later Dave came into the sitting-room. I was hunched on the couch sobbing brokenly, and I could see he was furious with me.

'Chrystal, it is not your place to speak to clients in that way,' he said angrily.

'Well, it's not his place to treat a dog in that way,' I sobbed.

'Next time, just stay out of it.'

'I won't. I'll *never* keep quiet about something like this,' I cried.

Eventually we both calmed down.

'Did you put him down?'

'Yes, I had to. It had gone too far.'

Later that afternoon Dave suggested that we go for a drive. He said I needed to get out. As he drove, I stared miserably at the passing countryside. It was dry and barren and ugly. For once I could detect no beauty in it. Everything was ugly. Sunk in a pit of misery, I was relieved when we finally returned home.

Physically and emotionally I had reached a very low point. The heat was oppressive and over the last few days veins had ruptured in the crooks of my arms.

'You need to get away from this heat for a while,' Dave remarked that evening.

'Yes, but how?'

'I think you should fly down to your mom for a couple of weeks.'

'We can't afford it.'

'We'll have to. And I think you should see your doctor while you're there.'

He made the flight bookings. I would fly from Matsapa Airport the following Monday and return twelve days later.

A few days after that the baby moved for the first time. I was standing under the bauhinia tree, inhaling the scent of the flowers and watching Dave dig in the garden, when I felt a flicker of movement in my stomach. I gazed down at it curiously. Had I felt something or was it my imagination? Then it happened again, like a delicate butterfly fluttering to get out.

'Dave.'

'Yes.'

'Come here.'

'Why?'

'I think it's moving.'

'What's moving?'

'The baby.'

Dave rushed over and placed his hand on my stomach. There it was again! Suddenly everything seemed more real.

The Monday of my departure arrived. Heartsore and tearful, I hugged each dog and cat. Whippy looked as if she was about to burst into tears too and I gave her a double hug. From the window of the aircraft I watched Dave standing at the barrier. He looked so alone. And I was missing him already.

My mother and Aunt Nova met me at Port Elizabeth airport. My home town was an hour's drive away.

My old room welcomed me into its arms like a comfortable well-worn sweater. Blossom was sitting on my bed when I entered. He stared at me for a few seconds before giving a raucous Siamese cry. Gathering him up into my arms, I hugged him until he squawked. He helped me unpack. Wherever I was busy, he was busy. When everything was unpacked we sat down on the bed together. He stared at me for a long time.

'Why did you leave me behind?'

'We thought you wouldn't enjoy the long trip by car.'

'You took the others.'

'Yes, but they were used to travelling.'

'I was with you long before they came.'

'Yes. I know.'

'Will you take me this time?'

'Yes. Oh Blossom, I'm so sorry.'

'I've missed you.'

'I've missed you too.'

Later, as I rested on the bed, I laid him on my stomach. As he felt the baby's movements, he gazed at me quizzically with his squinting blue eyes. That night he cuddled up next to me, lying on his back with all four feet in the air. He was nine years old now. I had longed for him in Swaziland and knew that there had been a gap in my heart which only he could fill. A special Blossom place, like an empty seat in a full auditorium with a sign on it saying 'RESERVED'.

Over the next few days I relaxed. It was the tail-end of winter in the Eastern Cape and the air was cold and crisp.

Already I was feeling better and I considered not bothering to see the doctor. But Dave had been adamant, so on the Thursday I made an appointment. My doctor was out of town for a few weeks and I was given an appointment with his partner, whom I knew and liked.

My cousin Mike had lent me a car for the duration of my stay and I drove myself to the consulting rooms. Dr de Goed looked concerned when I mentioned the ruptured veins. Silently, he examined my eyes with his ophthalmoscope. I lay on the examination bed as he listened to the baby's heart.

'These are nasty bruises,' he remarked, pointing to my side. I glanced down. There were two large blue-purple patches on the other hip to the one on which bruises had previously appeared.

'That's strange. I wonder where they come from?' I murmured thoughtfully.

'Chrystal, I want to run some blood tests. I'm sending you to the pathologists. I should have the results by Saturday.'

The pathologist's laboratory was in another part of town and as I drove I felt a bit anxious. What were they testing for, I wondered uneasily?

The rest of that day and the next Blossom and I relaxed in the garden. On the Saturday morning the phone rang. It was Dr de Goed. 'Chrystal, I want to see you. Can you come in straight away?'

'Straight away?'

'Yes, the results of your blood tests have just arrived. They are very abnormal.'

'In what way?'

'I'll explain when I see you. Try to get here as soon as possible.'

Dr de Goed was seated at his desk and as I sat down

opposite him, he looked up at me with a serious face.

'I want you admitted to hospital immediately.'

'Why?' I asked, staring at him blankly.

'Your platelet count is 70 000.'

'What should it be?'

'Around 250 000.'

'What does this mean?'

'Platelets cause your blood to clot. If you start bleeding, we may not be able to stop it. A platelet count of 25 000 can result in spontaneous haemorrhaging throughout the body. Even with 70 000 you are at high risk and a hospital bed is the safest place for you if something should go wrong.'

'Oh.'

'I'm referring you to a specialist physician in Port Elizabeth. Once you are admitted he will run some further tests.'

'Yes.'

'Try not to worry too much, we'll sort this thing out.'

I left his office in a daze. It took me five minutes to find the right key to unlock the driver's door. I sat behind the wheel with my mind churning. This was supposed to be a holiday and now suddenly I was being hospitalised. This is the pits, I thought, the absolute pits. And Dave wasn't there.

No Escape

It was as if someone had stood up on a stage and shouted, 'LET THE NIGHTMARE BEGIN!'

And it did.

Within two weeks, despite heavy doses of cortisone, my platelet count dropped to below 5 000. I underwent a bone marrow test for leukaemia. It was negative. Dave flew down from Swaziland and after discussion with the physician it was decided that I should consult specialists at Johannesburg General Hospital. It was closer to Swaziland and, being a teaching hospital, had state-of-the-art equipment and medical personnel who were the top in their fields. Taking Blossom with us, we flew to Johannesburg where Erica and Jonathan collected us at the airport.

Johannesburg General Hospital is colour-coded and huge. Completely overwhelmed by its size, my first thought was that someone like me could get lost in there. And not be found for days.

Coloured stripes run along the walls, branching off in different directions. Each department has its own colour. We made our way to Outpatients and explained the situation to the administrative assistant. She ushered us into a consulting room.

'Dr Baker will be with you shortly,' she said.

Five minutes later, a tall, well-built, youngish man entered. He had golden brown hair and piercing blue eyes in a strong face. He reminded me of a lion. His eyes had a sparkle, like Philby's eyes, only blue. We introduced ourselves and handed him the letter from the specialist in Port Elizabeth. He read the letter in silence and then looked up at me.

'When last did you have a platelet count?'

'On Monday. It was below 5 000.'

He looked grim. 'Well, the first thing I'm going to do is to check those platelets.'

After drawing blood from me, he asked us to return in an hour. There was an area on the ground floor where refreshments were available. He suggested that we wait there.

Dave and I sat down at a table with a cup of tea. Before the hour was up Dr Baker appeared. He pulled up a chair and sat down with us.

'You have a platelet count of 15 000,' he said, looking serious.

'Oh, it's gone up then,' I exclaimed, pleasantly surprised.

'Yes, but it's still dangerously low.'

'Maybe the cortisone is working now?'

'I think we have to be sure of that before you return to Swaziland. If you start haemorrhaging there they may not have the facilities to deal with it.'

I accepted the truth of what he was telling me. But oh, I so badly wanted to go home! Home to Whippy and the others. To walk in the shade of the forest and smell the bush in the early morning. To watch the sun go down behind the hills. I looked around me at the artificial lighting and the air-conditioning. I thought my spirit would wither and die here. Not even a breeze on my face.

'What do you suggest?' I asked resignedly, knowing what

was coming.

'I want to admit you to hospital and do a daily platelet count to make sure it continues to rise. It is imperative that we get that platelet count up before you give birth. It's highly dangerous for you to be walking around. What if you were to fall?'

'All right,' I sighed and Swaziland disappeared over the horizon, tail drooping sadly.

'Now,' he said briskly, 'go home and get your things together. I'd like you in the ward by six o'clock this evening. I'll see you there.'

Late that afternoon I said a tearful goodbye to Blossom.

His sky-blue eyes gazed deeply into mine. *'You're going away again?'*

'Yes, but it shouldn't be for long.'

'I wish you wouldn't.'

'I know, but I can't help it.'

'What about me?'

'You're going home to Swaziland, you'll like it there.'

'Will I?'

'Yes, I'm sure you will.'

I would never see him again.

I cried bitterly all the way to the hospital. I was admitted to a ward in the antenatal section. Antenatal was orange. Dave left after a while as he and Blossom were flying to Swaziland very early the next morning. The inevitability of saying good-bye hung heavily over us and it was better to get it over with.

Dr Baker popped in to say that he and the rest of the team would see me in the morning. He saw that I was upset and so he stayed and chatted for a while. Later, as I lay in the dark listening to the muffled sounds of the night staff going about their work, I wondered what was causing the low platelet count. Could I have picked up something from an animal I had handled? Maybe Splittie was right and monkeys did carry disease. Apart from the baby monkey, I had also had contact with two adult monkeys fairly recently . . . My mind drifted back to the incident.

A young man had telephoned Dave. He had a male monkey which he had reared from a baby and as it grew older it had become more and more attached to him. Fairly frequently he had to go away on business for a few days at a time and when this happened the monkey refused food and water until his return. This was a very worrying situation.

To complicate matters further, he had recently acquired a girlfriend and the monkey was becoming increasingly jealous of her and showing a tendency to bite. It was rather unnerving for the girlfriend, especially when a romantic hug from the young man prompted the monkey to sink its fangs into her legs. Hardly moonlight and roses.

The young man had heard of an adult female needing a home and he wondered if a mate was the solution. He wanted to introduce the two under veterinary supervision, in case matters got out of hand.

Dave agreed and suggested our garage as a suitable venue to eliminate a territorial reaction. The next day the young man and his girlfriend arrived with the two monkeys in separate cages.

Curiosity overriding good sense, I entered the garage with the group, closing the door behind me. People who speak of monkey business have no idea what it's really like. Dave opened the female's cage first and after a while she emerged timidly and sat on top of the cage, showing no inclination to explore. Then the young man opened the male's cage and the monkey business hit the fan.

There was a *THUMP* as he sprang out, grunting, and charged straight at the female, a lascivious leer on his face. With a horrified look, she ran straight up Dave's body and on to his head. As the male leapt crazily for Dave's head, she jumped on to mine. By the time he crash-landed on my head, she was already on the girlfriend's, clawing at her beautiful long dark hair in total panic. Rape and pillage were definitely on his mind and she was having none of it.

We stood in stunned silence as they played leapfrog from one head to another.

'Ahhh,' I shrieked, as the male clawed my neck. He was strong and very excited.

The heat in the windowless garage began to build up and, with it, the pungent aroma of monkey. We were all sweating profusely, and not necessarily because of the heat.

After a while the male seemed to become a little less aggressive, his leaping less frenzied, and I realised that in his bombastic way he was showing off. Suddenly the girl-friend said weakly, 'I think I'm going to faint . . .' and sank gracefully to the floor.

The young man rushed to her assistance and Dave and I were left staring at each other, round-eyed, each wearing an adult monkey on our heads. Like exotic hats.

'I need air,' came a faint moan from the floor.

With some difficulty, we managed to get the monkeys back into their respective cages. Opening the garage door, the young man half-carried his girlfriend outside. Dave and I stumbled out after them, hair standing straight up on our heads as if lacquered in place, reeking of monkey glands and urine and covered in scratches.

When the girlfriend had recovered the couple left. The young man said he thought it had gone quite well and he would continue the familiarisation process at home. The girlfriend remained silent.

'I don't think that relationship is going to last,' I muttered, as we watched them drive off.

'Well, at least they didn't bite each other.'

'What do you mean? Why would they bite each other?'

'Chrystal, I'm talking about the monkeys. Who are you talking about?'

'The young man and his girlfriend.'

Very early the next morning I was awakened by bustling nurses switching on the ward lights. My eyes shied away from the bright fluorescent lighting and before I was properly awake, a nurse waved a small glass vase at me and said, 'Urine sample please.'

The ward had six beds but only one other was occupied. Opposite me lay a young woman suffering from placenta praevia and depression. Her parents had taken me aside the previous evening and asked me to keep an eye on her. I was not quite sure what they meant by that, but I watched her anyway. She didn't talk much, only moans and heavy sighing.

Just after 8 o'clock, the medical team arrived and Dr Baker introduced me to Dr Sevitz, the other gynaecologist on the team. Thin and short in comparison with Dr Baker, he had dark hair and spectacles and the shy look of an intellectual. I liked him immediately.

My first impressions of Dr Baker and Dr Sevitz were very positive. They came across as intelligent and concerned. In the days and weeks that followed, I was never to change this opinion, only add to it, as their kindness and sense of humour became more apparent.

They went over me with a fine toothcomb. As I slumped back against the pillows after they left, I thought that I could not fault them for thoroughness.

Being in hospital was like being in a giant cocoon and one day just merged into the next. My platelet count remained at 15 000 for three days and then on the fourth, it dropped.

As Dr Baker drew the vial of blood, he said, 'What is it going to be today?'

'I think it's dropping again.'

'Why do you think that?' he asked, looking concerned.

'I don't feel right today.'

'You know, theoretically, a patient cannot feel a drop in platelets.'

'Oh.'

Two hours later, he was back.

'Your count is 10 000,' he said, shaking his head.

Dr Sevitz arrived with the senior gynaecologist from the other team. There were two teams, I had discovered. They decided to increase the cortisone dosage from 60 milligrams to 120 milligrams per day.

Now every morning I had to swallow twenty-four tablets. It took a long time. When I tried to swallow two at a time only one would go down my throat, while the other would hide slyly in my mouth and start dissolving. This must be the bitter pill that people talk about, I thought.

I phoned Dave from the callbox on the first floor to tell him about the count.

'How is Blossom?' I asked.

'He's fine.'

'Is he mixing with the other cats yet?'

'No, not yet.'

Something about the conversation disturbed me. Dave didn't sound himself.

A few days later, I was moved to a bed next to the window and another patient was admitted. Shannon was young, about seventeen. She was short, with dark hair and a cheerful disposition. It was nice to have company, the depressed placenta praevia having been discharged the day before. Still looking depressed.

Shannon was a different kettle of fish. Talkative and bouncy, she reminded me of a chirpy Cape robin.

To my amazement, I overheard her telling the social worker that she was suicidal. After the social worker had left, Shannon confided that she wasn't suicidal, but lonely and broke.

Strangely, Dave hadn't phoned the ward since my phone call to him four days earlier and so I phoned him again. After chatting for a while, I said 'How's Blossom?'

'Fine,' he said.

I waited for him to elaborate but he kept quiet.

'Dave.'

'Yes?'

'There's something wrong. What is it?'

There was a silence and then, 'Chrystal ... Blossom's gone.'

'Gone?'

'He escaped the same night I brought him home. I've been searching for him ever since.' As he spoke, his voice broke and we both started crying.

When Dave arrived home, he had closed Blossom in the spare room, as we had decided. What neither of us knew was that one window catch in the room was faulty and would swing loose at the slightest touch. As we had never used the room, except for storage, we were not aware of this. Some time during that night, Blossom had touched the window catch and walked out through the open window into the Swazi veld. Dave had searched and called, early in the morning and again in the evening, but there was no sign of him.

'Why didn't you tell me?'

'Your mother asked me not to.'

'She shouldn't have done that, it's better for me to know.'

'I haven't phoned because I couldn't stand lying to you when you asked about him.'

'It's not your fault, it would've happened even if I had been there. But please, just keep calling for him every day.'

'I do, whenever there's a break I walk the veld and call. The trouble is he doesn't know me so well.'

I walked back to the ward, devastated and heartbroken. All I wanted was to go home to Swaziland and find Blossom. But I knew I couldn't, not without risking our baby's life.

My platelets were sticking stubbornly at 10 000, despite the high cortisone dosage. The previous day Dr Baker and Dr Sevitz had been accompanied by a man whom I had not seen before – an oncologist, I discovered later.

Standing around my bed, they discussed the possibility of chemotherapy treatment.

'And the side effects?' asked Dr Sevitz.

'Well, there might be some hair loss, eyelashes and eye-brows perhaps,' the oncologist answered and then caught my eye as I glowered at him from the bed. I liked my eyelashes. Looking embarrassed, he drew Dr Sevitz aside and lowered his voice, muttering something about 'Checking with America'.

When he and Dr Sevitz left, Dr Baker remained at my bedside. Looking at me, he raised his eyebrows. I raised mine in return. I might as well use them while I still have them, I thought.

'Have you gathered what that was about?'

'Not quite.'

'They want to give you chemotherapy.'

'Why? I don't have cancer.'

'It causes an increase in platelets, although we don't know why, exactly.'

'Oh.'

There were a lot of things that we didn't know why, exactly. We didn't know why, exactly, the platelets were being destroyed. Despite a battery of tests, no specific disease or condition had been pinpointed. The official diagnosis at the time was 'ITP' or 'Idiopathic Thrombocyto-paenic Purpura'. Translated, this meant haemorrhaging under the skin for no known cause. It meant nothing really.

'Our medical panel have discussed your case and feel that a splenectomy is necessary,' Dr Baker told me. 'But they are reluctant to perform surgery while your platelet count is 10 000.'

'Oh.'

'If the chemotherapy can increase the platelets to a safer level, then they can operate. How do you feel about surgery?'

'I'm not sure. What about the risk to the baby?'

'There are risks, but it would be safer for the baby if we operated now, at this stage of pregnancy, than if we waited a month or more.'

Dr Baker left and I lay there thinking of a splenectomy Dave had performed on a greyhound in Swaziland.

I stood by during the op, to keep an eye on the blood transfusion and also to fetch anything he or Esther needed, as they were both working sterile.

As he prepared to remove the spleen, Dave said, 'Chrystal, bring a bowl.'

I rushed over with a large stainless steel bowl. As he lifted the spleen, he realised that it was enormous and shouted, 'GET A BIGGER BOWL'.

'Where? There isn't a bigger one.'

'From the house . . . GET ONE FROM THE HOUSE,' he growled impatiently. He was always a bit Jekyll and Hyde-ish during surgery.

In the house I grabbed a big plastic bowl and, just in case, took a bucket along too. In the end Dave used the bucket. The spleen was that big. Despite the transfusions and drips, the dog went into shock. Sadly, it died the next day.

Walking a Different Valley

Two student nurses were having an argument next to my bed about my urine sample.

'You must test it immediately, it mustn't be allowed to stand,' the one was saying.

'But I did, I tested it as soon as I saw it here.'

'Yes, but it may have been standing for more than five minutes.'

'Mrs Sharp, at what time did you produce this sample?'

'I'm not sure,' I mumbled, still half asleep.

'Was it five minutes ago, or ten minutes ago?'

'About seven,' I said deviously.

'Really Mrs Sharp, you must call us as soon as you've produced the sample.'

'OK.'

Just then, Dr Baker popped his head around the door to say that I would be receiving my first chemotherapy treatment later that morning. A sister from the oncology department came to set up the drip and inject the Vincristine into it. I lay there not feeling any different, except that after a while I noticed that I had double vision. When the drip was finished the ward sister called Dr Baker to remove it.

'How are you feeling?'

'Fine.'

'No side effects?'

'Not really. Just slight double vision.'

'Double vision?' he looked surprised.

'Yes, but it's not too bad.'

'You know, in theory, the drug is not supposed to cross the blood-brain barrier.'

'Oh.' As I looked up at Dr Baker, I could see more than one of him.

What theory would I mess up next, I wondered?

The windows in the ward were kept locked because of the air-conditioning and I felt stifled by the lack of fresh air.

'Nurse, could you open a window for me? I'm feeling a bit claustrophobic.'

'I'll have to ask Sister.'

'Thank you.'

Five minutes later she returned to tell me that the Sister did not have the keys to the windows. They were kept by the Floor Supervisor. They were trying to locate the Supervisor to obtain a key. Before long she was back, triumphantly waving a key. She unlocked the window next to my bed and slid it open.

'Just remember, when you want to close it, don't slide it all the way into the frame, it's self-locking and we have to return the key immediately.'

Shannon and I rushed to the window and, leaning on the sill, gazed out over Johannesburg. It was city air but, even so, it was air in motion. A gentle breeze ruffled my hair, I closed my eyes and was transported back to Swaziland. Walking the path down into the valley, Splittie marching ahead of me and, just beyond her, Whippy. I could see Dave's back, slightly stooped, as he checked the path for snakes. Philby was shouting excitedly to Carrots that he had spotted a leopard.

Suddenly the daydream was shattered as two student nurses entered the ward.

'Back into bed please, ladies, the medical team is on its way,' said one, looking worried.

Why was she looking worried, I wondered idly, as we left the window and climbed into bed. One nurse stood chatting to Shannon while the other moved to the window and facing me, leaned back against it and began sliding it into the frame. I opened my mouth to protest, but I was too late. With a loud click, the window locked firmly into place.

'Oh no . . . now look what you've done . . . you've locked the window and they've only just opened it for us,' I moaned, almost grinding my teeth in frustration. She rolled her eyes at me in a meaningful way. Nonplussed, I stared back at her as her eyes flicked to Shannon and then back to me. Then I understood. They thought Shannon was suicidal and we were on the fourth floor.

When they left, I turned to Shannon accusingly. 'They think you're suicidal, that's why they've locked the window.'

'Do you think so?'

'Yes. Can't you tell them that you're not?'

'No, then they'll discharge me. They're only keeping me here because I'm suicidal.'

'Well, are you?'

'No.'

Four days after the chemotherapy Dr Baker brought me the good news. My platelet count had risen to 25 000. I could see he was pleased, but I wasn't so sure. We were entering a new dimension now. This was confirmed just before lunchtime, when a tall thickset man, balding and bespectacled, strode into the ward and up to my bedside.

'Mrs Sharp?'

'Yes.'

'Good morning. I'm Dr Pickford and I'll be removing your spleen tomorrow.'

Time came . . . and time went . . . without my knowledge. Five hours went missing. I never found them again.

Only my eyes were alive, there was nothing else. No thought, no movement, no emotion, no pain . . . nothing. I lay there like an abandoned house, deserted, hollow, only the structure left standing. Shutters and doors banging, the sounds echoing eerily through empty rooms.

Then I was moving. Through endless dark tunnels first in one direction, then turning sharply in another. Aware of people behind me and at my side as, quickly and silently, we negotiated the tunnels, the silence broken only by the swish of the gurney's wheels. In the distance I saw a pinpoint of light and as we moved towards it a door swung open. Daylight flooded the tunnel as I was pushed into the ward.

Someone in a theatre cap bent over me, looking into my eyes. It was Dr Baker. I looked back at him, dully.

'It went well . . . and don't worry, your baby's fine.'

Deep inside, a tiny spark flickered into life.

'And look, your husband's here.'

Dave was standing at the end of the gurney, his face grey and drawn, tears welling in his eyes. Wordlessly, we stared at each other.

Nurses lifted me on to a bed. Dave stood at my side, holding my hand as I drifted in and out of consciousness. Once I opened my eyes to see Dr Pickford looming over me. I caught snatches of conversation. 'Blood loss . . . transfusion . . . risk of going into labour.'

Through a mist I saw Dr Sevitz and Dr Baker speaking to Dave.

Then they were at my side. 'We have to leave now. You'll be in Dr Gravehill's care,' said Dr Baker, gesturing towards a short man standing next to them.

'Dr Graveyard?' I slurred, confused.

'Dr Gravehill,' he said firmly.

I floated off.

A shaft of dying sunlight pierced the leafy canopy enveloping Whippy in a golden glow as she paused, waiting for me to catch up. Her body was illuminated, transformed for a few seconds into a radiant sculpture. As I drew level with her she left the light and drifted on through the shadows at my side.

We moved silently on moist rotting vegetation, the only sound an agitated rustling of treetops high overhead. The trees, ancient sentinels, joined hands to keep the wind out. Light was fading fast, hollows in the trunks forming orbs of darkness, deep black eyes observing our passage.

Moving between the tree trunks I became aware of a third presence in the forest. Filled with menace, it padded stealthily behind.

'Hurry, we must get home,' I whispered to Whippy, increasing my pace. She turned to gaze past me, eyes widening as the air swirled and a hot hand clasped my wrist.

The jerk unlocked my eyes. I saw a white form standing next to me. A nurse taking my pulse. Beyond her, Dave, Erica and my cousin Beryl were gathered around the bed.

'Oh, you're here too,' I mumbled.

'We've been here all the time,' Erica said.

My body was a slab of lead, heavy, immobile.

I slept.

Fleet-footed, we fled through the veld like wild creatures. Around the marshland and up the hill through waist-high grass towards the huge prehistoric boulders. Their brilliant orange and green lichen beckoned in the distance. A safe beacon. Arrow and Strider raced ahead as Whippy and I followed, panting breathlessly, lungs burning. Where was Sally? I glanced behind. No Sally. Only the towering incandescent wall of flame gaining rapidly. If only we could reach the stones. We'd be safe on the stones. Heat seared my back as the fire devoured the veld behind us. A monstrous creature with flickering tongue and insatiable appetite.

And then it was inside me, blazing in my abdomen and chest.

Groaning, I awoke.

I was in labour.

They managed to halt the labour but the next morning I couldn't breathe properly. It had come upon me gradually, but by the time Dave arrived I was struggling.

'Dave, please call the Sister, I can't breathe.'

She took one look at me and whipped an oxygen mask over my mouth and nose, plugging it into the oxygen supply on the wall behind my bed.

I felt totally helpless. There was no strength left in me. They had taken it out with my spleen. Dr Gravehill arrived with a physiotherapist. I blotted my copybook by calling him 'Graveyard' again and he looked annoyed. He had gingerish hair and a defensive personality.

'Dr Gravehill . . . *please* . . . Mrs Sharp.'

I was sorry, but my mind was in a fog. Sometimes the mist would clear and I was lucid, at other times it was so thick I couldn't see my hand in front of my face. At times, hallucinating, I stared into Philby's eyes, their sparkle absent as he stared back gravely.

The physiotherapist listened to my lungs with a stethoscope, while I inhaled and exhaled.

After a while she turned to Dr Gravehill. 'Two-thirds of the left lung has collapsed and one third of the right. Mrs Sharp, I'll organise a machine that will exercise your lungs but you're too weak now, we'll have to wait, maybe tomorrow.'

I existed inside my head, my body a mutinous army resisting all commands. I felt so tired but each time I attempted to sleep a feeling of suffocation would overwhelm me and eventually I stopped trying.

On the fifth day after the splenectomy I was transferred back to Antenatal.

When we emerged into a corridor with an orange stripe on the wall, I knew I was almost there. I was lifted on to a bed and I saw that I was in a private ward. The nurses stayed for a while to chat, but when they realised I was too breathless to speak they left. That evening the Sister brought my spectacles and I could see more clearly. Later, lying in the semi-dark room and gazing about me, I saw three skulls in the curtains. I blinked, but when I looked again they were still there, staring down with hollow eyes. As if they had a message for me. I removed my spectacles thinking that perhaps it was better not to see. All day I had been looking forward to sleeping. Now I was going to sleep.

'Mrs Sharp . . . Mrs Sharp . . . wake up.' Someone was shaking me. Wearily, I opened my eyes. Two nurses were bending over me and the light was on.

'We're so sorry to wake you, but your breathing is very erratic.'

'What do you mean?'

'It was very shallow and then stopped completely and then started again. We were worried.'

'Oh.'

The rest of the night was spent staring into space. I was so tired.

On the Wednesday morning, like a sick dog, I lay down to die. I could not fight any longer. My body felt as if it had been through a mangle. Without sleep since the Friday afternoon, I had passed beyond the point of exhaustion. Way beyond. I started weeping and found that I couldn't stop, it just seemed to gather momentum.

The Sister and nurses, obviously troubled by this development, popped in and out every half-hour or so.

'Mrs Sharp, what is it? Why are you crying?'

'Please tell us what we can do to help.'

'Are you in pain?' they asked anxiously.

Mutely, I shook my head as the tears seeped down my face.

Just before lunchtime a man wearing a black suit and white dog-collar ambled into the room. He was an elderly man with white hair, a bushy white beard and twinkling blue eyes. He looked like Father Christmas, I thought, staring at him through a veil of tears.

'Sister sent me to you. I'm Father Saviour from the Anglican Church. My dear, I know you're not Anglican but I've come to pray for you.' Taking both my hands in his, he began praying in a soft gentle voice.

'The Lord is my shepherd, there is nothing I shall want.'

Like an eagle on high, my mind drifted on the words of the prayer.

'He leads me beside quiet waters, he restores my soul.'

I was kneeling on soft green moss, gazing into the cool brown stream near the old house. As the ripples smoothed and stilled, my own face stared back at me and, next to it, the faces of Whippy and Philby looking troubled.

When he came to the words 'Even though I walk through the valley of the shadow of death', a warm glow started at my toes. It spread slowly upwards through my entire body and peace flowed in my veins like a healing balm.

Filled with a golden light, I closed my eyes and allowed it to wash over me.

'Would you like a cup of tea?'

I opened my eyes to see a nurse pushing a tea trolley.

'Oh. Where's the priest?'

'What priest?'

'Father Saviour. He said he was from the Anglican Church.'

'I don't recall seeing any priests here today. Would you like a cup of tea?'

'Yes, please. Nurse, what time is it?'

'It's teatime, 4 o'clock.'

I had slept for four hours.

The Sister entered as I was sipping the tea. 'Ah, you're looking better than you did this morning.'

'It was the priest you sent to me.'

'What priest?'

'He said the Sister sent him.'

'Oh? Well, it may have been another Sister, it wasn't me.'

'Oh.'

Back on Track

A week after the splenectomy, my platelet count had risen to 30 000. When Dr Baker brought me this news, I listened glumly.

'To go through all this, just for 5 000 platelets,' I remarked bitterly, shaking my head. 'It hardly seems worth it.'

They called in the oncologist, Dr Bart. Further chemotherapy was advisable, he said, but only once I was stronger. One week later I was discharged from hospital with strict instructions. Under no circumstances was I allowed to return to Swaziland. I would have to attend the outpatient oncology clinic once a week and, depending on my platelets, undergo chemotherapy.

Erica and Jonathan came to fetch me. Erica brought one of the dresses I had bought in Manzini. It hung on me like a sack.

Following them through the big sliding doors, I stumbled in the sunlight, dazzled by its brilliance. After weeks of fluorescent lighting it seemed too bright, almost artificial.

As Jonathan drove, I stared at passing motorists and pedestrians. People were going about their daily business in much the same way as they had been on the day I was admitted. And yet so much had happened in between.

Everything seemed new. The sun, the sky, the grass, the

trees – all had a sparkle to them. My thoughts wandered back to the day I had led Whippy from her hospital cubicle into the sunshine. Now I understood.

'We're going to stop at a nursery to choose plants for the garden,' Jonathan said.

'That's fine,' I replied.

As they strolled between rows of plants at the nursery, I sank down on to a rock, feeling weak. The air was warm and still and bees purred from blossom to blossom. A reddish-gold cocker spaniel ambled up to me, looking hopeful. Reaching out, I ran my fingers through its silky coat which gleamed like burnished copper in the sunlight. We sat together in contemplative silence. My emotions were in limbo, as if my body had freed itself from the hospital leaving my emotions trapped behind. In the twilight zone of its cocoon.

'Chrystal, we're ready to leave,' Jonathan called. 'Are you OK?'

'Yes, I'm fine.' Giving the dog one final lingering caress, I rose slowly.

Something in me was saying, 'Wake up . . . and smell the bush.'

Shortly after the second chemo treatment as an outpatient, something marvellous happened. Erica's daughter Vanessa contracted chickenpox. On my next visit, I mentioned this to Dr Bart.

He stared at me. 'You've surely had chickenpox as a child?'

'No.'

'You've *never* had chickenpox?' he asked incredulously.

'No.'

'*You have to get out of that house!* Your immune system is totally suppressed.'

'I'll have to go home to Swaziland then.'

'Do you not have other family in Johannesburg you could

stay with?'

'No,' I said, lying through my teeth.

Although actually it was true. I did not have family in Johannesburg. Beryl lived in Pretoria. An hour away. Johannesburg was riddled with Dave's relatives but he hadn't asked about them.

'When can you leave?'

This was more like it, I thought enthusiastically.

As we drove through the border post at Oshoek, I inhaled deeply and Swazi air filled my lungs. Further on, halfway between Mbabane and Manzini, a great big sob built up in my chest. I battled to contain it, but despite my efforts it burst out and Dave glanced at me anxiously.

'It's all right,' I reassured him with tears streaming down my face. 'These are tears of joy.'

I was going home. It was the 26th of December and I was going home. I had flown from Matsapa Airport to Port Elizabeth early in October, almost three months ago.

As we pulled into the bumpy driveway and Dave got out to open the gate, my heart swelled in my chest. We drove in, coming to a halt outside the kitchen door and, right on cue, Joseph opened the door with a grin stretching from ear to ear. As we beamed at each other, Whippy, Mandy, Arrow and Strider erupted from the kitchen, almost bowling him over. Whippy managed to reach me first. Squealing and licking me ecstatically, she lavished on me all the love she had been saving up. Just for me. The others surrounded me, barking excitedly. One by one, I hugged each of them.

Looking up, I saw Philby standing in the doorway. I walked over to him.

'Philby, it's me.'

At the sound of my voice his eyes lit up and there was that old sparkle. I cuddled him to my chest and he started purring. As a rule, Philby never purred. That was Carrots' speciality. Philby's talents lay elsewhere.

'*That was a long holiday,*' he said reproachfully.

'Believe me, it was no holiday.'

'*You've missed all the excitement.*'

'What excitement?'

'*There was a lion in the garden.*'

'Oh?'

'*Yes . . . but don't worry, it ran off when it saw me approaching.*'

'I'm not surprised.'

One by one, I found all the cats and hugged and stroked them. Except Seafood, who took one look at me and hid in the garden. And Alfie. Without me to watch for an aura, his fits had got out of control despite the daily medication. When Dave saw that he was becoming brain damaged, he asked Brendan to come and euthanase him. Him and Sally. Her hind legs had finally given in completely.

Splittie greeted me testily, wriggling impatiently as I tried to cuddle her.

'*Don't DO that.*'

'I'm sorry.'

'*Where have you been all this time?*'

'Why? Did you miss me?'

'*No.*'

'Why do you ask then?'

'*We might have needed you.*'

'I thought you didn't need anyone?'

'*Not me. The others.*'

Nuggie and Carrots rubbed themselves all over me, complaining bitterly.

'They didn't feed us at the right time.'
'Sometimes it was LATE at night.'
'And it wasn't enough.'
'Never mind, you can have double helpings tonight, OK?'
'OK.'
Dave brought my suitcase from the bakkie and slowly, pausing every now and then to gaze at the hills through the bedroom window, I unpacked. I was pulling a pair of his thick long socks over my legs when he came into the room to tell me someone had just arrived with a sick dog.

'What are you doing?'
'I'm going to look for Blossom.'
'Chrystal, just wait a while and I'll come with you.'
'I can't wait.'
'Which way are you going?'
'I think I'll go past the avo trees and straight down into the valley, not along the path.'
'I don't think you should go alone.'
'I'll be all right.'
'When I've treated the dog I'll join you.'

Closing the dogs in the house I set off, walking slowly. Once past the avo trees, I continued straight on down a rocky slope. Climbing over the barbed wire fence I crossed a narrow dirt track and then continued down another steep incline into the valley. The surface was short grass and easy to walk on.

The bottom of the valley was a concertina of hills, small hills and folds, one wrinkle after another. There was not another living person in sight. As I called 'BLOSSOM . . . BLO . . . SSOM,' the words echoed back at me eerily. An eagle floated on air currents in the distance, the absolute stillness was broken only by my calls. I felt as if I was the only human being on God's earth. I followed the gullies, calling his name. I was getting tired but each time I came to a rise I thought maybe he's in the next one . . . or the next. And I walked on.

Finally I stopped and sat down on a ledge in a hollow place between two hills. Two lizards emerged from a crack in the rockface and peered at me nervously. The hollow was like a suntrap and after a while, feeling too hot, I stood up to make my way back.

As I stood, I realised that I had walked too far. It was as if my batteries had suddenly gone flat. My legs were shaking with weakness, knees threatening to give way.

How could you be so stupid, I thought.

For some reason, throughout all those weeks in hospital, I had hoped that as soon as Blossom heard me call, he would come hurtling from the bush into my arms. That somewhere nearby he was crouching, waiting for my voice to bring him home.

But it had been too long.

Summoning every ounce of will power left in me, I started walking. Eventually in the distance I saw the track and slowly made my way towards it.

Like a chameleon on all fours, I inched up the hill. As I stumbled on to the track I heard 'Chrystal' and there was Dave, climbing over the fence. Then he was at my side.

'I walked too far,' I said, starting to cry. Half-carrying me up the rocky slope he lifted me over the barbed wire.

'I would've come sooner, but Brendan and Mary arrived,' he apologised.

In the sitting-room I dissolved on to the couch.

Brendan and Mary sat on the opposite couch, watching me with concern.

'How are you, Chrystal?' Mary asked in her soft Irish accent. For some reason, these words were a signal for the opening of sluice gates in a dam that had been threatening to burst. I started sobbing – raw, broken, raucous sobs. I cried as I'd never cried in my life before.

I cried for Blossom. I cried for Alfie and for Sally and for the fear and pain and the loneliness of the past three months. I heard Brendan say to Dave that maybe they should leave. Through my sobs, I said, 'No . . . don't go, just let me cry, when it's over I'll be fine.'

And I was. Shedding all the pent-up emotions of the past months in that catharsis of tears, I picked up the traces of my life and moved on.

Taking Leave

When I was discharged from hospital, the medical team had expressed the fear that the baby or I could present with problems after the birth, possibly requiring medical treatment or surveillance for some time. With the cause of the platelet problem still unknown, they could not foretell what the future held, for either of us.

On the drive back to Swaziland, Dave and I had discussed the matter at length. In circles, around and around, always arriving back at the same point. We were afraid that we might be separated again for months. Neither of us felt emotionally able to handle another separation and the financial implications were also frightening as we were barely making ends meet. Long-term medical costs were not within our means. Desperate to stay but accepting that we had no real choice, we gave our landlady one month's notice. We would leave Swaziland for Johannesburg at the end of January.

On New Year's Eve we were invited to a party at Brendan and Mary's home. Several of their friends were Irish too and the laughter and conversation flowed until well after midnight. It was a wonderful evening. Sitting back in a chair listening to the lilting Irish voices, I wondered what the new year would bring.

On our way home at one o'clock in the morning, I turned to Dave. 'Shall we stop at the dump?'

Nodding, he swung off the road on to a bumpy dirt track. In his search for Blossom, Dave had heard of a colony of semi-wild cats living in the vicinity of a wrecked car dump. Knowing that lost cats have a tendency to gravitate towards other cats, he had visited the dump before, but only during the daytime.

So there we were, in the first hours of the new year, in a graveyard of old abandoned cars. It was a surrealistic scene, the hollow broken hulks squatting forlornly on the ground, bathed in brilliant white moonlight.

At intervals I called, 'Blossom . . . Blossom.'

There was no answer.

It was officially summer now and the heat was taking its toll. Day after day the searing sun beat down and the earth cracked in protest. Plants wilted and dried, kept alive only by the frequent tumultuous storms. After a storm the heat would build up again until the very earth seemed to sweat, giving off the vapour of the rain it had just absorbed.

Even at night there was little relief and we would toss and turn in bed.

'What does "Hot as Hell" mean?' Carrots asked me one day.

'Where did you hear that?'

'From Philby.'

'He would know, yes.'

'What do you mean?'

'Never mind.'

The swimming pool became a cool oasis in an overheated world and the hills resounded with the splashing of bodies entering the water. Dogs, cats, humans; only Esther refrained although I think she was sorely tempted. In the evenings we would swim before supper and again before bedtime.

At night, lying on my back in the water, my buoyancy enhanced by my inflated abdomen, I would float quietly to and fro, gazing up at the stars and listening to the sounds of the veld. It was a far cry from lying in a hospital bed under the glare of fluorescent lighting, but the natural beauty of our surroundings was like an intravenous drip feeding my spirit.

A few days after the party, Whippy and I crossed the highway to walk in the forest. As always, it was as if we were entering another world, a silent shadowy world where footsteps made no sound on layers of moist rotting leaves. A tranquillity of stately old trees watched our progress and I wondered idly if the king had ever used the house in the forest. Perhaps long ago, to entertain visiting foreign dignitaries. I daydreamed colourful scenes of twinkling lights and the sibilant murmur of foreign accents.

As we approached the house, my friend the royal guard stepped out on to the veranda. I called and waved in greeting and he came down the steps to meet me.

'Morning,' I smiled as Whippy raced up to him, tail whirring in circles.

Stroking Whippy gently, he grunted, 'You been away?'

'Yes, I was sick.'

He nodded sympathetically. Explaining about Blossom, I showed him a photograph. Had he seen him?

He shook his head. As I was leaving he mentioned that Arrow and Strider had been roaming the forest recently. This was very disturbing news, and I turned towards home deep in thought.

As Whippy and I strolled down the driveway, Dave

emerged from the kitchen clutching something in his arms. It was a baby goat. One of our clients had found it wandering next to the dirt road looking lost and confused. Fearing that it would be struck by a passing vehicle, they had brought it to us.

It was white and tan and very small. Dave went off to Mrs Pocock to see if she could supply us with goat's milk. He returned with the milk and a feeding bottle.

Sizing up the situation, the little goat decided that Dave was its mother and it stuck to him like a leech, never leaving his side. When Dave took one step, it took three . . . to keep up.

Later that afternoon Splittie stomped out of our bedroom, muttering under her breath.

'What's the matter with you?' I asked curiously.

'*I can't take it any longer,*' she huffed, marching past me.

'What? What can't you take?'

'*The wildlife in the bed.*'

'WHAT?'

I found Dave lying on the bed on his back, snoring. Next to him with its head on the pillow, also snoring, was the baby goat.

The room was redolent with the pungent odour of goat. I walked back down the passage to the sitting-room where Splittie was reclining moodily on the couch, paging through her copy of *The Female Eunuch*.

'Move over,' I said, lying down next to her.

'*AH . . . so you can't take it either?*' she smirked.

'No, it's not that. Anyway it's livestock not wildlife.'

'*They smell the same.*'

'Hmmm.'

I lay there thinking of Nanny Pocock. Thank heavens I had been firm about not taking her. The picture of her lolling on the couch eating popcorn had been replaced in my mind by an image of her hulking great body lying between us on the bed. With four feet in the air, and snoring raucously.

The telephone trilled in the sitting-room and I rushed to answer it. It was the manager of a local dairy farm. I went to call Dave. Several of their cows had died mysteriously over the past few weeks. All the tests Dave had run in collaboration with Brendan at the laboratory had proved inconclusive. Now there was another cow down.

I was busy in the kitchen when he came to find me. 'They want me to transport the cow to Onderstepoort,' he said.

Onderstepoort is the veterinary faculty near Pretoria.

'When?'

'As soon as possible. We hope that whatever is causing the deaths may be detectable in the live animal.'

'What did you say?'

'I said it would depend on you. How do you feel about being alone here overnight?' Joseph was away for a few days.

'I don't mind. When will you return?'

'Tomorrow afternoon, if all goes well.'

'Don't worry about me, I'll be fine.'

Dave's main concern was the fact that we were very isolated on the smallholding – our closest neighbour was on a farm about one kilometre down the dirt road. I assured him that if there were any problems, I would contact Brendan. Late that afternoon he set off in a farm truck with the cow on the back.

As darkness fell that evening the storm which had been threatening all afternoon finally erupted. The sky was streaked with lightning and thunder rumbled and echoed through the hills as the rain came sheeting down. At 8 o'clock I noticed that the lightning was moving away into the distance, although it was still raining heavily.

Suddenly the dogs began barking at the outer kitchen door. Wading through them, I opened it, expecting to find someone on the doorstep. There was no one. As I peered out through the rain, I could see the headlights of a vehicle parked on the perimeter of the parking area. I waited, but nobody emerged. Feeling a little uneasy, I closed the door and locked it.

I stood in the kitchen deep in thought. I wondered what I should do. I was reluctant to leave the house and approach the vehicle in the darkness. Just then, the dogs began barking furiously and jumping up at the door. I opened it again to find a Swazi man standing outside.

He nodded in greeting and, pointing at the vehicle, said, 'They want doctor.'

'The doctor isn't here at the moment. What is the problem?'

I couldn't see the occupants of the car at all, the interior was in total darkness and visibility was hampered by the teeming rain.

'You come ask them.'

'No, I'm not coming out, they can come here,' I said firmly, trying to conceal my unease. Turning away, he walked back through the rain. If he was with them, why did he not know what the problem was?

Two minutes later he squelched back to the door. 'Dog is sick,' he stated.

'How sick?' I asked.

He shrugged his shoulders but made no comment.

'Look, I'm sorry, but the doctor is not home. Those people

must come here to me and tell me exactly what the problem is.'

Nodding heavily, he ambled back across the parking lot. This time he did not stop at the vehicle but walked past it. Totally mystified, I watched him disappear from sight up the driveway. What on earth was going on?

Still no one emerged from the vehicle and after a few minutes I once again closed the door and locked it. Slightly on edge, I began preparing the dogs' supper. Every few minutes I peered through the kitchen window. I could still see the car's headlights reflecting the rain.

Ten minutes later there was a heavy knock on the door and after a moment's hesitation, I opened it cautiously. Standing outside were a middle-aged Swazi couple.

'Good evening,' they said.

'Good evening.'

'We need to see a vet, our dog is very sick. Your security guard said he would fetch him, but we waited and nobody came.'

'What security guard?' I asked, perplexed.

'Your security guard, the man you were speaking to.'

'He's not our security guard, I thought he was with you.'

'No. He was walking down the driveway when we drove in. He said he worked for the doctor.'

We stared at each other blankly.

'I've never laid eyes on the man before in my life,' I said.

'Neither have we.'

I gave them directions to the vet in Mbabane and they left. I decided to sleep with the lights on.

At 10 o'clock I was lying in bed reading when there was a knock on the kitchen door.

'Oh no . . . not again,' I muttered.

Fighting my way through barking dogs, I opened the

door a crack.

It was John, the farmer from down the road and his son, Gavin.

'Hello, Chrystal.'

'Hello.'

'Sorry to disturb you this late.'

'That's OK.'

'We've just been checking on a cow in the field near the farmhouse and we heard a cat meowing. We wondered if it was your Siamese.'

'Oh.'

'Perhaps Dave can come and have a look?'

'Umm, Dave's not here, but I'll come.'

They looked doubtful. 'It's in the veld, over a barbed wire fence.'

'Don't worry, I'll manage.'

I dressed hastily. Fortunately the rain had ceased. The night sky was clear, aglow with stars and with the moon to illuminate our path. We set off up the driveway and on to the dirt road. I walked carefully on the muddy road, afraid of slipping. John and his son were wearing boots. After walking some distance we could see the lights of the farmhouse and John stopped.

'It was down there towards the dam that we heard the sound.'

The barbed wire fence was waist high. Grabbing my elbows they hoisted me over it.

On the other side I immediately sank ankle-deep into marshy mud. As we made our way down the slope towards the dam, I sank deeper and deeper until eventually I was calf-deep in mud and it required some effort to take a step forward. Like quicksand, the mud gripped my feet, releasing them each time with a reluctant *plop*.

We stopped at the thick bank of reeds surrounding the water and I called, 'BLOSSOM . . . BLOS . . . SOM,' and then waited. The silence was broken only by the clicking of frogs.

'BLOS . . . SOM . . . BLOSSOM.' Nothing. After ten minutes we gave up and made our way slowly up the slope.

When I got home I decided I had better have a bath before getting into bed. Apart from my legs, which were black up to the knees, splatters of mud were clinging to my face and arms. Not even my hair had escaped.

Dave returned at lunchtime the next day.

'How was your night?' he asked, hugging me.

'Fine.'

Two weeks before we were due to leave, Strider was knocked over and killed on the highway.

I was busy in the kitchen when I noticed Brendan's government van pull into the parking area, coming to a halt just outside the surgery. I strolled outside to greet him.

'Hello, Chrystal. Is Dave around?' he asked. He looked serious.

'Yes, he's busy sorting things in the surgery. Just go in, he's alone.'

Wondering why he appeared so sombre, I watched him open the door and disappear inside. Something was wrong. Brendan was normally so cheerful.

Within seconds he and Dave emerged. They walked over to the van, opened its rear doors and stood staring inside. I went over to them as Dave was leaning into the van.

'What's happening?' I asked.

Straightening, he turned to me, looking grim. 'It's Strider, he's dead.'

Looking past him, I saw Strider's beautiful, sleek, lifeless body. Curled up on his side, not a mark on him. I reached out to stroke him. His body was still warm to the touch.

'Are you sure? He's still warm,' I asked, my voice breaking.

'Chrystal, I'm so sorry but he is dead. I checked when I found him,' said Brendan.

He had been on his way to a stock inspection when he noticed Strider lying next to the road below the forest. He checked for any sign of life and finding none, he had loaded him into the van and brought him home.

'If only he could've held on for two weeks,' I wept. 'He would've been safe in Erica and Jonathan's enclosed garden.'

Dave and I had been afraid that he would come to grief. From a very young age Strider had mirrored his mother's joyful exuberance, her zest for life. However, whereas Whippy always kept us within sight, Strider would hurtle off recklessly despite our efforts to restrain him, usually taking Arrow with him. He had a spirit that could not easily be contained, and he had paid for it with his life.

We buried him in the shade of the avocado trees, it was cool and peaceful there.

Like two boxers, we reeled under the blow of his death, trying to absorb it so that we could continue with the task of winding up the business, packing our possessions, and storing memories.

The last glorious sunset beyond the hills, the last walk along the path down into the valley. Breathing in the smell of raw earth in the vegetable garden, the elusive wafting scent of the bauhinia blossoms. Trying to retain it, somewhere inside.

We were relieved that Esther had managed to find employment with a medical doctor and our landlady, Mrs Barker, had asked Joseph to stay on as caretaker-cum-gardener for an indefinite period.

One day, a week before our departure, I lay down on the mossy grass beneath the willow tree. Through the cascading fronds I gazed up at an endless blue sky. Suddenly the endless blue sky was obscured by Carrots and Philby. They stood, one on either side of me, peering into my face.

'Is something wrong?' I asked, sitting up.

'*Carrots is worried,*' Philby said carelessly.

'What is Carrots worried about?'

'*This place called Johannesburg, he wants to know about it.*'

'What would he like to know?'

'*Will there be walks in the bush?*'

'No.'

'*What about wildlife?*'

'Not of the four-legged kind.'

'*No snakes?*'

'No.'

'*Leopards?*'

'I'm afraid not.'

'*WHAT IS THERE, THEN?*'

'Oh, many things. Traffic, pollution and, of course, criminals, lots of criminals.'

'*Maybe we could start a criminal collection. You know, catch them and keep them.*'

'Others have tried and failed.'

Rising from the grass, I walked up the veranda steps towards the sitting-room.

Behind me I heard Philby whispering to Carrots: '*What*

we really need is a gun.'

'THERE WILL BE NO GUNS!' I shouted over my shoulder.

Before we knew it, the day of our departure was upon us. By the early hours of the morning we had finished packing the bakkie, planning to leave at dawn, while the day was still cool.

Joseph stood in the middle of the parking area waving forlornly as we drove slowly through the gate and up the driveway, with all our worldly possessions loaded into the back of the bakkie. Also loaded into the bakkie were three dogs and five cats.

I leaned from the window, looking back at Joseph and waving until he was out of sight.

There was much that we were leaving behind.

A Cap in the Hand

Erica and Jonathan had suggested that we stay with them until we were able to rent a house of our own. We moved into a flatlet above their double garage. It consisted of one very large room containing a double bed, two comfortable chairs and a kitchen sink unit. The drawback was that the toilet and bathroom were situated in the main house downstairs. This wouldn't have been a problem if it hadn't been for the staircase.

The staircase to the flatlet was a staircase straight from hell. Made of steel and resembling a fire escape, it shuddered violently as one moved from one step to the next and I envisaged it coming off the wall one day. With me still on it. Dave, Erica and Jonathan assured me that it was quite secure but I wasn't convinced. When I descended I held grimly on to the railing, terrified of tripping and catapulting out into space. My overactive imagination supplied a picture of me hitting the ground and bursting like a berry. Splat.

At eight months of pregnancy, my centre of gravity was no longer somewhere between my hips. It was ensconced just behind my belly button. Suddenly I knew why very pregnant women show a tendency to lean backwards when they walk.

We had a harrowing experience the day after our arrival,

caused by our very own personalised chaos factor, Philby. Erica had warned us that their neighbours at the back owned a German Shepherd with a notorious reputation for killing cats. When we arrived in Johannesburg, we confined the cats to the flatlet for the rest of the day. The next morning I decided to take them into the garden on leads, one at a time, in relays.

Everything proceeded fairly smoothly. Carrots, Nuggie and Seafood trailed around after me quite happily and when I removed the lead, they remained cautiously at my side.

Splittie flatly refused to walk on a lead. *'They're for dogs.'*

'Nonsense, cats use them too.'

'Not THIS cat. I've never been so humiliated in all my life!'

Sighing heavily, I allowed her to inspect the garden without the lead. Then it was Philby's turn.

He stretched his neck obligingly as I fastened the collar and clipped on the lead, and as I strolled through the garden he remained at my heels. An observer would have concluded that this was a highly trained cat. It was all a façade. He was playing me like a fish on a line.

After a while I sat down on the grass and unclipped the lead. He appeared not to notice and continued sniffing the grass next to me. Dave emerged from the flat and I glanced up at him momentarily, before looking back at Philby. Who was no longer there. Startled, I looked around and to my horror saw him nipping over the fence into the property at the back – the cat-killer's territory.

'DAVE,' I shouted. 'Come quickly!' I pointed to Philby's tail which was disappearing into the thicket of bare branches on the other side of the wire.

Dave came hurtling down the staircase and as he ran towards the fence I raced inside to find Erica.

'Erica, phone your neighbours! Ask them to take their

dog inside, Philby is in their garden.'

Erica hurried to the phone and I rushed back outside. Dave was trying to move towards Philby but was hampered by the twisted tangle of branches. Fortunately the dog hadn't spotted either of them yet and I didn't dare call Philby, in case it alerted the dog to his presence. I heard the neighbours calling, 'Savage . . . SAVAGE . . . come.' After a few minutes, they shouted that the dog was closed in the house, just as Dave reached out to grab Philby.

With a neat twist of his body, he eluded Dave's grasp, snaked through the branches, jumped over the fence and sidled up to me, eyes sparkling. Resisting the hysterical urge to give birth immediately, I grabbed him roughly by the scruff of his neck and marched him up the staircase and into the room. Dumping him on the floor and slamming the door, I tottered back down to help Dave climb over the rickety wire. He was covered in bleeding scratches from the branches and was muttering 'that bloody cat' at regular intervals.

We returned to the room and collapsed into the two chairs. Speechless and despairing, we gazed at Philby. He gazed back at us, round-eyed.

'Why are you looking at me like that?'

'I specifically told you not to enter that property. You deliberately disobeyed me.'

'I only wanted to see.'

'See what?'

'What a cap-killer looks like.'

'A cat-killer.'

'You said cap-killer . . . I thought he killed caps.'

'He kills cats . . . CATS!'

'Oh . . . sorry, if I'd known . . .'

That evening I telephoned my mother. 'Mom, can you

take care of three cats until we find a house of our own?'

'Yes, which three?'

'Philby, Carrots and Seafood,' I said, with bated breath.

'Yes, of course. How will you get them to me?'

'We'll fly them down.'

The next day I contacted an animal travel agency and explained that it was a matter of urgency. Fortunately they had two cat cages available and one was big enough to accommodate two cats. Later that day they phoned to confirm the flight booking and to inform me that the cats would be collected early the next morning.

When the Animal Travel van arrived, the cages were placed on the grass at the bottom of the staircase. I carried Philby down first, closing him inside the larger cage and then I closed Carrots in with him. Gingerly descending the stairs yet again with Seafood clutched in my arms, I bent down to put her into the smaller cage. Then I heard the sound of sniffling coming from the other cage. Peering through the wire, I saw that Carrots was upset.

'What's the matter? Why are you crying?'

'*I don't want to go to an animal shelter,*' he moaned pathetically.

'What animal shelter? What are you talking about?'

'*You're giving us to an animal shelter.*'

'Who told you that?'

'*Philby.*'

I glared at Philby, who appeared to be transfixed by a butterfly on the grass.

'Philby, don't always lie to Carrots.'

He turned towards me and suddenly I understood. His eyes were dull and sad, so terribly sad.

'Philby,' I said gently, 'I'm not giving you away, I'll never give you away.'

'*Oh.*'

'I'm flying you to Granny Fay, for your own safety.'

'*Oh,*' he said, perking up. '*Flying?*'

'Yes.'

I opened the cage doors to give them all one final hug and, as they were being loaded into the van, I heard Philby whispering gleefully to Carrots. Something about the Concorde and breaking the sound barrier.

Shortly after taking the decision to leave Swaziland, Dave had applied for an assistantship in a multi-man practice in Johannesburg. They would have preferred him to begin immediately but were prepared to wait until we relocated.

Two days after we arrived in Johannesburg, he set off early in the morning for work. Dr Sevitz and Dr Baker wanted to see me for a general check-up and platelet count and later that week Dave deposited me at the hospital on his way to the practice.

The orange of Antenatal greeted me cheerfully and I felt as if I'd never been away. The sister paged Dr Sevitz who was consulting in the clinic on the ground floor.

'Good morning, Mrs S,' he said cheerfully, striding up to me, white coat flapping. 'You're looking well.'

After the examination, he drew blood for the platelet count and suggested that I come along to the clinic with him while we waited for the results. He said it would simplify matters after the birth if I was registered there. 'You know, initially you came in through the back door, so to speak,' he smiled.

Breaking into a trot to keep up with him, I followed him to the ground floor.

The clinic was a hive of activity, with women in various stages of pregnancy all over the place. It was like being at a pregnancy convention. Summoning a nurse, Dr Sevitz asked her to take me to the registration area and I followed her to a large open area which formed part of the foyer at the hospital entrance. Running along two sides of the room were counters and desks, forming an L-shape. Facing these were several rows of chairs in which people were sitting waiting. There were long queues before the three counters and the nurse stood me in one of them.

'You need to queue here for a number,' she said. 'When your number is called, a registration clerk at one of the desks will register you and open a clinic file.'

'Thank you,' I murmured.

'Please return to the clinic as soon as you have been registered. Dr Sevitz will be waiting for you.'

'Yes.'

After thirty minutes I reached the head of the queue and the young man behind the counter took my name and handed me a slip of yellow paper. I looked at it with misgiving. I read '93'. It was going to be a long wait.

I sat down and looked around me. I noticed that everyone's eyes were riveted on the line of desks, their faces wearing expressions of quiet desperation. Turning to the elderly woman seated next to me, I asked how long she had been waiting.

'Since 7.30 this morning,' she replied, glancing at me briefly, before fixing her eyes firmly on the desks once again. I looked at my wristwatch, it was 9.30. She had been waiting for two hours. I noticed that pregnant women were being called to the desk on the far left.

An hour later the young nurse returned. 'Have they not called you yet?' she sighed impatiently.

'No, they're busy with the 30s and I'm number 93.'

'Dr Sevitz will be finished with his other patients soon, I wish they'd get a move on.'

'Me too,' I said feelingly. I was not used to sitting for long periods, my backside was numb and my back ached. I needed to use the toilet, but I was terrified that '93' would be called as soon as I disappeared around the corner. So gritting my teeth and crossing my legs, I waited ... and waited. By now I knew that my face mirrored the expressions on the faces around me as I stared fixedly at the desks, willing them to call '93'.

And then at last it happened.

'Ninety-three,' sang out a thin, bespectacled young man from one of the desks. I rushed over to the desk with indecent haste, almost tripping over my feet, and sat down facing him.

'Which clinic are you registering for?' he asked.

'Antenatal.'

'Antenatal?' He looked confused.

'Yes, I'm pregnant.'

'I'm afraid you're at the wrong desk,' he shrugged apologetically. 'Antenatal patients are registered over there.' He pointed to the desk on the far left.

I stared at him blankly. 'How did I end up here then?'

'I'm not sure. There are two batches of numbers, one for Antenatal and another for the remaining clinics. I think you've been given a number from the wrong batch.'

'Can't you just register me anyway?' I asked in a voice bordering on hysteria.

'Unfortunately not. This computer is not programmed for Antenatal.'

'What shall I do?'

'You'll have to queue at the counter again for a new

number.'

Thinking bitter thoughts, I rejoined the queue at the counter and after an eternity, faced the same young man who had given me the slip of yellow paper.

'I was given a wrong number. I need an Antenatal number.'

'Who gave you the number?'

'You did.'

'Did you tell me you were pregnant?'

'No. You didn't ask.'

Rolling his eyes heavenwards, he tossed a slip of green paper on to the counter. I glanced at it. Number 30.

I walked wearily over to the chairs nearest the Antenatal desk. As I sat down, I heard the woman at the desk call out, 'Number eight'. Sighing heavily, I decided to find a toilet. It was becoming a matter of urgent necessity.

As I was returning from the toilet, I almost bumped into the young nurse from the clinic. 'I've been looking for you everywhere,' she exclaimed accusingly.

'I needed to use the toilet.'

'Dr Sevitz is waiting for you. Have you been registered?'

'No.'

'But you've been here for two hours!'

'I know that.'

She stood for a moment, deep in thought. Then she grabbed my arm. 'Come, we can't keep Dr Sevitz waiting.'

'Mrs Sharp has not been registered yet,' she informed Dr Sevitz.

'After all this time?' he asked incredulously.

'It's not that easy to come in through the front door,' I uttered gloomily.

'Never mind, we'll just have to organise your registration ourselves. Your platelet count results are in, they are 80 000.'

I nodded gratefully.

'Come with me, Mrs S, I want you to enter your name for antenatal classes. I know you're having a Caesarean section but you can still fit in a few classes. It'll help with the breathing.'

He led me to a small counter where a middle-aged woman was busy sorting papers.

'Mrs Ball, please put Mrs Sharp on the list for classes. You'll have to open a clinic file for her, she doesn't have one. Mrs S, I must leave now, but I'd like to see you again next week.'

Mrs Ball stared at me. 'Why do you not have a file?'

'It's a long story.'

'Really, this is most irregular. It's all very well for Dr Sevitz to tell me to do it, but it's not that simple.'

'I know that.'

'You should go through the correct channels,' she said, looking annoyed.

'Believe me, I tried.'

'Right,' she huffed. 'You'll have to give me your particulars. When is your baby due?'

'In three and a half weeks, at the end of February.'

'*Three and a half weeks!* And you're only coming for classes *now*?'

'Yes.'

'Really, you've left it very late, very late indeed.' She glared at me disapprovingly.

'Yes.'

Leaning against a concrete pillar in the underground parking lot as I waited for Dave, I reflected on the morning's events. The hospital administration system appeared to be rejecting me, as if I were a transplanted organ. I hoped I wouldn't have to have too much to do with it.

Philby and Co. had flown to my mother on a Tuesday. On the Friday evening she telephoned me in a state.

'Chrystal, Carrots is missing!'

'Carrots?' I asked, taken aback. Carrots had never disappeared before.

'Yes, he wasn't here for breakfast this morning and I've just returned from work and he's nowhere to be found.'

'That's very strange.'

'Yes, I'm worried sick. I'm not sure if I can cope with these cats. The day after they arrived Philby went missing, but he came home at 5.30 that afternoon.'

I kept quiet. Apart from the dagger strapped to his thigh, the cat was wearing a wristwatch.

'Mom, what is Philby doing?'

'Well, he ate his supper and since then he's been sitting on the boundary wall staring into the Burketts' garden.'

'You must look in the Burketts' garden.'

'I called over the wall, it's too dark to see anything now.'

'Mom, please phone them and ask them to look.'

'Chrystal, I've tried. There's no one home, the house is in darkness.'

'Oh.'

Deeply worried, I replaced the receiver. Philby's disappearance and reappearance at 5.30 was normal behaviour. But Carrots? Something was wrong. Very wrong. That night I lay tossing and turning in bed, picturing Carrots lying dead or injured somewhere.

The next day, just after lunchtime, Erica called up to me. 'Your mother is on the phone.'

'I've found Carrots.'

'Is he alive?'

'Do you know where he was?'

'Mom, IS HE ALIVE?'

'Yes.'

She had tried, without success, to contact the Burketts early that morning. Returning from work at lunchtime, she had tried again and this time they were home. Mrs Burkett said she would search the garden immediately. She found Carrots locked in the cellar under their house.

There was not an iota of doubt in my mind as to who had taken Carrots into that cellar.

'Look, there's a door under that house.'

'Oh.'

'Maybe a Troll lives there, let's have a look.'

'I'm scared of Trolls.'

'Carrots . . . GET A LIFE!'

'OK then.'

'You go first, I'll guard your back.'

The Underlying Heartbeat

Opening my eyes in the darkness, I looked at the window. The faint glow of street lights filtered in from outside. My body felt cold and wet. Running a hand down my side, I discovered that it *was* wet, sopping wet. That's odd, I thought. Then a ripple of pain flickered across my abdomen and I knew.

Staring at the illuminated window, I uttered a silent prayer and then, with a deep sigh, I shook Dave gently.

'Dave, wake up, please.'

'Wha . . . what is it?' he mumbled sleepily.

'It's started.'

'What . . . what's started?'

'Labour, I'm in labour.'

He sat bolt upright in the bed, peering at me through the gloom. 'Are you sure?'

'Yes.'

'But it's two weeks too soon.'

'Yes, I know.'

He sprang up, switching on the light and fumbling for his clothes. 'I'll go downstairs and phone the hospital.'

Clanging noises drifted into the room as he hurried down the iron stairs and I remained sitting on the side of the bed, terrified. Whippy stood watching me, sensing my fear. She

182

laid her head in my lap and I stroked her gently. After a while I stood up and started to dress.

At 4.30 in the morning the highway was deserted and the bakkie hiccuped and spluttered along, as if sharing my reluctance to arrive. In the distance we saw the lights of the hospital rising up into the Johannesburg skyline and we turned off the highway and drove into the parking area at the Outpatients Department.

I stumbled after Dave through electronic doors into the quiet dimly lit interior. He spoke to the clerk on duty who lifted a telephone receiver and said a few words before replacing it.

Dave walked over to me. 'They'll be with us shortly,' he said. Within seconds a nurse appeared and we followed her down the corridor and through double doors into a large room. Soft lighting and low voices perpetuated the atmosphere of the dark hours, the tail-end of night, before the dawn brings light.

Curtained cubicles lined the walls, two of them with curtains drawn, the rest open. Each cubicle contained a bed. The nurse led us to an open cubicle. She handed me a surgical gown and asked me to undress and put it on.

I lay back on the bed, engulfed in the gown. 'Dave,' I said, 'they must phone Dr Sevitz or Dr Baker.'

'Don't worry. I'm sure they will.'

Dr Sevitz had emphasised the importance of being contacted if I went into labour while he and Dr Baker were off-duty. 'They must contact one or both of us immediately labour starts,' he had told me. 'We'll need time to take a platelet count and prepare for the Caesarean.'

The curtains twitched apart and a sister entered the cubicle accompanied by a dark-haired man wearing a white coat.

'Good morning, Mrs Sharp. I'm Sister Evans and this is Dr Cortini,' she said.

Dr Cortini smiled at me. 'Tell me, how far apart are the contractions?' he asked in stilted English and I realised that he was foreign. Italian, I thought.

Dave interrupted before I could reply. 'Dr Cortini, I wonder if you would phone Dr Sevitz and Dr Baker please? My wife has been under their care and they asked to be informed as soon as labour started.'

He smiled understandingly. 'Do not worry, we have experience in these matters.' He gestured towards the sister.

'No,' said Dave. 'You don't understand. My wife has ITP.'

'EYETEEPEE?' murmured Dr Cortini doubtfully. 'What is that?'

'Idiopathic Thrombocytopaenic Purpura. She is not allowed to give birth naturally. She must have a Caesarean section.'

Dr Cortini looked at us uncertainly.

'She has a low platelet count,' Dave continued. 'If the baby's platelets are also low, a natural birth process will cause it to haemorrhage into the brain.'

Sister Evans turned to me. 'If you've been treated here, you must have a hospital file?'

I nodded.

'Any instructions regarding you will be in the file. I had better find it.'

I nodded again and they left.

Dave and I looked at each other.

'He's foreign,' I whispered.

'That doesn't matter.'

'He can't speak English.'

'Yes he can.'

'It's broken English,' I hissed. 'And I don't think he knows what ITP is.'

'Chrystal, relax, it's just a minor language difficulty,' Dave said. But he looked very worried.

A young nurse came to take my temperature and blood pressure. As I lay there, the thermometer protruding from my mouth, a deep groan emanated from one of the closed cubicles, followed by high-pitched screams: 'IT'S COMING! IT'S COMING!'

All hell broke loose. As nurses ran to the cubicle, the double doors swung open and two porters pushing a gurney ran towards the screams. Within seconds they had bundled the woman on to the gurney and raced from the ward. We heard the screams fading into the distance.

With the thermometer still in my mouth, I gazed up at Dave, my eyes out on stalks. He attempted a nonchalant smile but I noticed that his eyes were bulging too.

After a while Dr Cortini returned. 'Mrs Sharp, we have some problems, we cannot discover your file.'

I stared at him in horror. The administration system was rejecting me again. I tried to remain calm.

'Dr Cortini?'

'Yes?' he said patiently. He was a kind man, I realised.

'I have been through much in this pregnancy. My spleen has been removed . . .' He opened his mouth to comment, but I continued '. . . Dr Sevitz and Dr Baker know my history. They asked specifically that they be contacted. Please just phone one of them. Please, please just phone them.'

He looked at me thoughtfully, then turned and walked to the office.

Within minutes he was back.

'They're on their way. Dr Sevitz has given instructions. You are to be moved to Labour Ward immediately and prepared for a Caesarean section.'

'Thank you,' I sighed in relief, close to tears.

Patting my hand reassuringly, he called a nurse. 'Please bring a wheelchair for Mrs Sharp.' Perched in the chair I was pushed through the doors and into a waiting lift.

The lift opened on to a brightly lit corridor. No dim lights here. Sisters and nurses moved around with a sense of purpose. It was a hive of activity and it occurred to me that this was the heartbeat of the hospital, the place where life began.

I was wheeled into a ward containing four beds, two of them were occupied. After I had been assisted on to the third bed, I looked around curiously. The ward seemed small and cramped and Dave said he'd wait outside for a while.

A blonde-haired woman in the far corner was moaning at intervals. Opposite me, a woman with long dark hair streaming over the pillows was breathing rhythmically: 'Huff huff huff . . . pause . . . huff huff huff'. She must have been to classes, I thought guiltily. Observing her closely, I began to imitate her breathing. 'Huff huff huff . . . pause . . . huff huff huff.'

Suddenly Dr Baker was at my side. 'Hello, Mrs S,' he said smiling down at me.

'Hello.'

'Why are you breathing like that?'

'Because she is,' I pointed to the long-haired woman.

He looked at her for a moment and then turned back to me, shaking his head in amusement. 'I think you should just breathe normally,' he said kindly.

'OK.'

'When Dr Sevitz arrives we'll take you into theatre.' A tall nurse pushed a trolley up to the bed and connected a drip on to the stand. Dr Baker inserted a needle attached to a blood collection tube and when this was full, he connected the drip. He handed the tube to the nurse, saying, 'Take this to the lab, tell them we need a platelet count STAT.'

I felt a sense of detachment, of isolation, almost as if it was no longer Dave and me facing this thing. It was just me and the gynaecological team. Gathering my strength about me like a cloak, my desire to communicate evaporated into a mist of dread. Dave stood quietly at my bedside holding my hand. He was facing his own fears.

A short while later, Dr Sevitz walked in. 'Morning, Mrs S. You've taken us by surprise,' he said cheerfully.

'Yes.'

'Your platelet count is 70 000.'

'Oh.'

These words sounded familiar. Then I remembered sitting opposite Dr de Goed and hearing him saying, 'Your platelet count is 70 000.' Ironically, we had come full circle.

Suddenly the pace of the treadmill quickened and I found myself in the waiting area outside the theatre.

This is it, I thought, scared out of my wits. Dave had requested permission to be in the theatre during the operation but this was refused. I suspected they were afraid that if things went wrong he would want to jump in and do the job himself. Their fears were probably justified.

As the theatre door opened to allow the gurney to pass through, we said goodbye. For a long moment I looked into his face, sure that I would never see him again. Then the doors closed behind me.

In the theatre, I was lifted on to a stainless steel table. Dr Baker stood at my side, his hands on my arm. I had a sense of *déjà vu*. This had all happened before.

This time, however, there was a green curtain on a stand placed next to the table. The curtain hung over my chest, preventing me from seeing my abdomen.

'What is the curtain for?' I asked suspiciously.

Dr Baker shrugged diplomatically.

'What is it going to be, Mrs S?'

'What do you mean?'

'A boy or a girl?'

'A girl.'

'Oh, why?'

'Because I want a boy.' I glowered up at him.

Someone was busy with my other arm and I felt a feather-light movement across my abdomen.

'What are they doing . . .' I started to say, but before I could finish '. . . behind that curtain,' there was nothing.

Rising up from the depths like a surfacing diver, my head broke through the water and I opened my eyes and blinked in the harsh light. I saw Dave looking down at me, his face tired and drawn. Taking my hand in his, he smiled and I sensed something beneath the tiredness, an inner excitement barely contained.

'We have a son and he's perfect.'

'Are you sure?'

'Yes, he's fine.'

I knew I should be feeling some deep emotion, but I felt like the main character in a drama who was inexplicably absent from the final scene, the climax. The song of a man who has come through. Without the singing. Closing my eyes, I succumbed to the lethargy that seemed to fill my entire body and mind.

Someone was shaking my arm. 'Mrs S, how are you feeling?' It was Dr Baker.

'Fine,' I mumbled with a thick tongue.

'Any pain?'

'A bit.'

'We've given you a strong painkiller, which is why you're still feeling woozy.'

'What time is it?'

'It's one o'clock.'

'When may I see my baby?'

'Haven't you seen him yet?' he exclaimed in disbelief.

'No, he's not here. I've looked.'

'Nurse, Mrs S has not seen her baby yet, please bring him to her.'

The nurse returned with a tiny bundle tightly wrapped in white flannel. She placed the bundle gently between my arm and my body and I peered down at his crumpled red little face. Wrapped up like a miniature Egyptian mummy, his face was the only thing I could see.

I stared at him, mesmerised, struggling to comprehend that this was the little person I had been carrying around inside me. The almost mythical being who had shared my trauma without comment. My underlying heartbeat. As I watched, his eyelids fluttered and suddenly he stared back at me with milky dark blue eyes. Having spent so long without commenting, he decided to do so now and a thin hiccuping cry emerged.

'Why is he crying?' I asked helplessly.

'I think he's hungry,' replied the nurse and before I could protest, she had whipped him up and disappeared from the ward. One minute he was there, the next minute he was gone. I was being rationed.

Dr Baker was still leaning back against the window, arms folded across his chest.

'His platelet count at birth was the same as yours, but we expect it to rise over the next few days. I nodded, cringing inwardly at the thought of that needle.

A short while later I was moved from the recovery ward to a private ward in the post-natal section. Here nurses washed me and dressed me in my own nightgown, and checked my temperature and blood pressure. When they had finished, I lay back, exhausted.

A voice was saying, 'Don't you think it's time you woke up?' Opening my eyes, I saw Erica beaming at me.

'Your baby is absolutely beautiful,' she said.

'Oh, where did you see him?'

'Chrystal, he's here, look.'

And he was. In a little cradle on a tall frame, right next to my bed.

'May I hold him?'

'Of course! He's your baby, silly.' She laughed and, lifting him up, she placed him in my arms.

I held him close to me for a long time.

When Dave arrived that evening, we stood next to the cradle staring down at the baby, who returned our gaze with serious interest. At 9 o'clock a nurse came to take him to the nursery. He would be monitored throughout the night, she said. Reluctantly we accepted the wisdom of this and handed him over.

'Love, I must leave now, it's been a long day. I'll see you tomorrow evening.'

Watching Dave leave, a surge of loneliness washed over me and I settled down to sleep.

At cockcrow the fluorescent lights flashed on, plucking me rudely from my dreams. A nurse handed me the baby and a bottle.

'He's hungry,' she said.

I sat back against the pillows, cradling him in my arms as he sucked contentedly. Before the Caesarean it had been decided that he would be bottle-fed initially, in case my physical condition after the operation was too precarious. He accepted the bottle readily and later when I did attempt to breast-feed, it was not a resounding success and the bottle stuck.

After breakfast, a nurse came to show me how to bath him and change his nappy. I was able to move around, albeit bent over. Soaping his perfect little body, I suddenly knew what his name was. It was Nicholas. Before his birth I had been reading a novel by Mary Stewart called *Touch Not The Cat*, in which one of the main characters was named Nicholas. Throughout the book Nicholas communicates on a telepathic level. Only at the end does the reader discover his identity. It seemed an appropriate name, somehow.

When he was sleeping, I carried the drip slowly down the corridor to the lounge area and settled down to smoke an illicit cigarette. As I sat there inhaling peacefully, a tall, thin young woman drifted in and sat down opposite me. An 'earth-mother', was my immediate thought. They wear natural fibres and health sandals. Her dressing-gown appeared to be hand-woven from goats' wool. Sniffing the air with nostalgia, I was transported back to Swaziland, and Splittie marching from the bedroom in high dudgeon.

Wrinkling her nose distastefully at the smoke, she began to chat.

'It's so fulfilling to give birth naturally, don't you think?'

I grunted noncommittally.

'We planned this pregnancy from conception to birth and it's been an AMAZING experience.'

'Yes, mine too,' I agreed wholeheartedly.

'And breast-feeding has made me feel so much more of a woman. Don't you agree?'

'I'm not breast-feeding.'

She looked taken aback.

'But I still feel like a woman.'

'Oh? Anyway,' she continued, 'we decided right from the beginning that I would refuse any drug or painkiller during the birth process,' she grimaced slightly as she shifted in the chair.

'Oh yes.'

'And even before conception, we ate only fresh fruit, vegetables and whole-grain cereals.'

'Really?'

'Yes. I only wish I could have my baby with me now.'

'Where is your baby?' I asked curiously.

'They have him in an incubator under lights,' she said, looking distressed. 'He's jaundiced.'

'Oh, I'm sorry to hear that. Maybe it was all the fruit and vegetables.'

'What do you mean?'

'Well, you know, all those growth hormones and insecticides.'

'But we bought our supplies from a health shop,' she said, looking shocked.

'Oh well, it should've been all right then.'

Just then, a young man and an older woman entered the lounge.

'Here are my husband and his mother,' she exclaimed in relief and the three of them moved to a group of chairs in the far corner. Glancing over casually, I noticed that he was wearing socks and health sandals. She was leaning over and speaking in a low voice and I heard the word 'vegetables' repeated several times. Suddenly she paused and, as one, they all turned and stared at me.

Smiling gently, I gazed back at them, round-eyed. It was pure Philby.

My thoughts drifted to Philby and I wondered how he and the other two were doing. Perhaps Seafood would develop more of a personality, now that she was separated from Splittie. We had decided to keep Splittie and Nuggie with us because Splittie, with her misshapen legs and suspicious nature was unlikely to venture far on her own and Nuggie suffered from chronic sinusitis which required antibiotics sometimes.

Poor old Nuggie. He loved to pretend he was a dog, walking at heel and bounding up to us obediently when called. Unfortunately, this was how Splittie treated him. Like a dog. She disliked dogs.

'There will be NO PLAYING, NO LICKING, NO PHYSICAL CONTACT AT ALL,' she stated categorically when Nuggie bemoaned the loss of his friends. *'And blow your nose while you're about it, it's disgusting.'*

Splittie's list of dislikes was long and detailed. It included Whippy, all other dogs, Italian epileptic cats, all other foreigners, baby monkeys, all other wildlife, goats, all other livestock, and strangers. Her list of likes was short and final: me, Dave and Seafood. Unfortunately, prior to Seafood's departure, even that relationship had become somewhat strained. Seafood had shown an increasing tendency to hero-worship Philby and Splittie had been horrified at this development.

'That cat is nouveau riche, he has no background,' she exclaimed disapprovingly.

Seafood would nod meekly in agreement, waiting only until Splittie's back was turned before she romped off gaily with Philby on yet another of his hair-raising adventures.

Rising carefully from the chair, I made my way slowly back to the ward. Would Splittie like Nicholas, I wondered?

After a few days in hospital, all I wanted was to go home.

To take Nic and go home and be an ordinary mother. Not a platelet count or a splenectomy or a Caesarean. Just a mother.

Everyone in the hospital was more experienced than me. They could all change nappies, feed and bath and burp better than I could. Often nursing staff would whisk Nic away to be checked by the paediatrician. I was not allowed to accompany him, I was told. A few days after his birth, they drew blood for another platelet count. I knew it was necessary, but I didn't like it.

Now I understood Splittie's attitude after the birth of her two kittens and I seriously considered springing from the bed and shrieking 'NO PHYSICAL CONTACT!' when nursing staff attempted to remove him. And I wouldn't have retracted my claws either.

'Ten days,' said Dr Sevitz firmly, when I enquired how long I would be hospitalised. Each morning I lay in wait for him, haggling and wheedling, presenting new arguments that had come to me during the night. After two days, he bowed to the relentless pressure.

'Eight days,' he said firmly.

On the seventh day after Nic's birth I was allowed to go home.

As the bakkie came to a halt in Erica and Jonathan's driveway, Whippy, Mandy and Arrow came running madly and, taking turns, sniffed at the bundle in my arms.

'Wait, I'll show you when we're inside,' I said, mounting the iron stairs with extreme caution. Nuggie and Splittie were sitting on the top step, looking excited. In the room they all gathered around me as I unwound the blanket, placing Nic on the bed.

Of course Whippy was in the front row. She ran her nose gently over his face and he didn't seem to mind at all.

'*He's beautiful,*' she sighed, eyes glowing with love.

'*Absolutely exquisite,*' Splittie murmured and I looked at her in surprise.

'*And he doesn't look at all like the other one,*' Whippy continued.

'Which other one?'

'*The little baby monkey.*'

'No, he doesn't, does he?'

Coming to a Head

Within days of bringing Nic home to the flat, I acquired the services of two nannies and a mother's little helper.

Whippy and Mandy vied for the positions of Chief Nanny and Assistant Nanny and I think Mandy won. She decided that since Nic was a chip off her old block (Dave), she would guard him with her life. Some mornings, when it was neither too hot nor too cold, I would place Nic in his carrycot in the garden. With an officious grunt, Mandy would immediately settle down on one side of it with Whippy on the other. They would watch his every movement with total concentration and if there was the slightest peep, Mandy would send Whippy upstairs with a message.

'*Mandy says his nappy is wet again.*'

'But it can't be, I changed it only ten minutes ago.'

'*Mandy says it is sopping wet and you must please come quickly.*'

'OK, OK, I'm coming.'

'*Mandy says Nic is hungry.*'

'So soon! I've only just fed him.'

'*She says can you please come now because he's crying.*'

'Tell her I'm on my way.'

Splittie dedicated her time to helping me. Never was a mother's little helper more critical.

'*Be careful with that pin, you're going to stick it right into him.*'

'I know what I'm doing. It's nowhere near his flesh.'

She would wait until I had the nappy on before stating smugly, '*You forgot the nappy liner.*'

'No, I didn't.'

'*Yes you did and you know what that will lead to.*'

'What?'

'*Nappy rash.*'

Sighing heavily, I would remove the nappy only to discover that I had in fact forgotten the liner and I'd have to put up with Splittie's smirks for the rest of the day.

After Nic's birth our lifestyle underwent a dramatic change. Days of striding through the Swazi veld under a blazing sun, or walking in the deep coolness of the forest, disappeared into the mist of the Lebombo Mountains. Crouching on cool wet moss beside a stream watching the antics of water insects for hours on end, was rudely replaced by kneeling on tiles, peering into a bath filled with dirty nappies. The nappies were pretty boring, they didn't do much.

Despite this, it was a time of consolidation. A period of calm after the storm of the pregnancy. Routine supplanted fear and pain, healing the physical and mental scars. We were in limbo.

But even limbo can be disturbed. One month after his birth, Nic and I attended a clinic near Erica's home.

'You have to go once a month, everyone does,' Erica told me firmly when I expressed reluctance. She was a highly qualified paediatric sister and she knew all about these things.

The clinic was situated in an old house just down the road. Gathering Nic up in my arms, we set off. As we walked up the stone pathway to the door, the sound of screaming

billowed out into the garden. Nic and I gazed at each other apprehensively. Inside it was chaos. Babies in various stages of undress were howling their lungs out, while mothers, red-faced and harassed, were trying to communicate with clinic sisters above the hellish noise.

'The milk doesn't agree with him,' one mother was shouting valiantly.

'Pardon?'

'THE MILK. It doesn't agree with him.'

'I'm sorry, can you speak up?'

'HICCUPS . . . HE GETS HICCUPS FROM THE MILK.'

Nic took one look at the scene, opened his mouth and emitted a piercing wail. As his wail scaled the heights, a sister approached.

'YOU MUST UNDRESS HIM SO THAT HE CAN BE WEIGHED,' she bellowed, her face puce with the effort of communicating above the bedlam.

I removed Nic's clothes while he screamed in tune with the other babies, my attempts to soothe him lost in the cacophony. As I approached the scale I was horrified to find that the previous baby had urinated in the tray.

'I can't put him in there, it's full of urine,' I protested.

The sister stared at me fixedly for a few seconds, then whipped a sheet of paper towel into the tray and haphazardly mopped up the pool.

'There, it's dry now, put him in.'

'It's not dry, it's still wet. Shouldn't you disinfect between babies?'

'It . . . is . . . not . . . necessary,' she hissed through clenched teeth.

Very reluctantly, I placed Nic in the tray and once she had recorded his weight, I squatted down awkwardly in a corner to dress him again. Every available surface was taken up by mothers dressing or undressing their babies.

As Erica opened the front door, I rushed past her and up the stairs into the bathroom. She followed me and watched, puzzled, as I ran a bath and popped Nic into it.

'What are you doing?'

'I'm bathing him. We won't be going there again,' I told her.

'Why not?'

'It was most unhygienic. He had to lie in a tray that was still wet with another baby's urine.'

'You're joking.'

'No I'm not. And they don't disinfect.'

Two weeks later we found a house to rent in Germiston, only ten minutes' drive from the veterinary practice where Dave was employed. According to our landlady, the house was in Germiston and the back garden was in Bedfordview, a neighbouring suburb. During the day, the cats and dogs basked in the sun of Bedfordview. At night they slept in Germiston.

It was quite a large house, with a long narrow kitchen and a sunny sitting-room which looked out on to the back garden. The dining-room was dominated by a huge table – so huge that we had to sidle along the walls to get to the French windows which led outside. There were three bedrooms, a bathroom with a sunken bath and a separate shower and toilet. The front garden was not fenced or walled and, from the start, we seldom used it. The outer kitchen door opened on to a paved area enclosed by a six-foot wall and one side of the garage. We had neighbours on two sides only as the house was built on a ridge overlooking a busy motorway in the valley below.

At night I would lie in bed pretending that the roar of the traffic was the roar of the sea in the Eastern Cape and picturing the waves thundering in one after another, white foam boiling and churning on to the moonlit sand. I would hear the sharp clattering of shells and pebbles as the foaming water was sucked back and absorbed into the sea. Like the water, I felt the pull of the Eastern Cape deep inside me. The inevitability of it.

One day just seemed to merge into the next. The daily routine of feeding Nic, bathing him, dressing him, cleaning the house, washing nappies and bottles, repeated itself without much variation. We were living in a very built-up area, with a garden so immaculate there was not a blade of grass out of place. My spirit felt boxed in. Even the rocks were arranged in straight lines or disciplined curves and they were rinsed off severely once a week by the gardener who came with the house. He was part of the deal. No gardener, no house. So although we could not afford it, we employed a gardener. The grass was mown to within an inch of its life and any weed with the audacity to rear its head was plucked rudely from the ground before it could even say, '*Hello, what's your name?*' I seriously considered concealing the weeds, but where? There was no place to hide in that garden.

I longed for the untamed wilderness of Swaziland, the sense of the primitive in land and sky, the thundering tumult of storms lashing the hills and the raw magnificence of vegetation in its natural state.

'There's nothing natural here,' I observed moodily, as I gazed down at the motorway, its rising fog of exhaust fumes trapped in the sunlight.

Kneeling on the ice-cold tiles, I leaned forward into the sunken bath and gave the nappies one final swirl. Then I lifted them one by one from the water and dropped them into the bucket at my side. Slowly rising to my feet, I straightened, groaning slightly, and stood for a few minutes flexing my body.

Two weeks after Nic was born I had noticed a slight stiffness in certain joints. It had gradually spread until most of my joints were stiff and aching, especially early in the morning. A few weeks later when I went for a final check-up at the hospital, I mentioned the painful joints to Dr Sevitz.

'Sometimes the pain is quite bad.'

He paused, looking at me thoughtfully. 'It may be connected to the fact that you're off the cortisone.'

'Will the pain disappear eventually?'

'I'm not sure. This is not a normal reaction.'

'So what do you suggest?'

'Mrs S, the head of our department has requested an interview with you today after my check-up. I think you should mention the joint pains to him. He might have an explanation.'

I made my way down the long passage to the Professor's rooms wondering what he was like. Prior to the splenectomy he had consulted with the Heads of Oncology and Surgery about my case, and had made the subsequent decisions. Despite this, we had never met. His secretary said that he was expecting me and ushered me into an office. A large grey-haired man was seated behind a very large desk. He rose as I entered and greeted me before seating himself once more. I sat down opposite him.

'Ah, Mrs Sharp, I wanted to meet you before we closed your file,' he smiled, looking at me curiously.

I looked back, equally curious. He was wearing a

yarmulka and a twisted lock of hair hung down on either side of his face.

'You had a rather traumatic pregnancy.'

'Yes.'

'How are you feeling now?'

'I'm fine. Except for my joints.'

'Your joints?'

'Yes, they've become rather painful.'

'Hmmmm,' he leaned back in his chair, looking pensive. 'Are they swollen at all?'

'No, just generally painful. When I've been bending over the bath washing nappies, it's difficult to straighten up.'

'Couldn't you use a nappy service?'

This was quite a novel approach. I stared at him blankly.

'We can't afford a nappy service, we have a gardener.'

For a few moments we regarded each other in silence. Then he seemed to rouse himself. 'Surely,' clearing his throat, 'your husband is a professional man, surely you can afford a nappy service?'

'Not really, I'm afraid. As I mentioned, we have a gardener.'

'Speak to him, Mrs Sharp. I'm sure he'll make a plan.'

'Yes,' I said, mystified at the turn this conversation was taking.

'Of course, the cause of your low platelet count has yet to be diagnosed. We are still in the dark as to why it occurred. Although there are several possibilities.'

'Mmmmm,' I nodded, recalling the possibilities that I had been tested for. Leukaemia, Brucellosis, Rheumatoid Arthritis, Systemic Lupus, Toxoplasmosis, to name but a few. All the tests had proved negative.

'Strictly speaking, having given birth, you are no longer a gynaecological case. I would suggest that if the joint pains continue, you see a specialist physician for more tests.'

At the word 'tests', my mind assumed the foetal position.

'If at a later stage a diagnosis is made, we would appreciate hearing from you.'

'Yes, of course.'

'Well, best of luck, Mrs Sharp . . . and do speak to your husband about that nappy service.'

'Thank you, I will.'

Why did I always end up having these Through-the-Looking-Glass conversations, I wondered as I left. It must be something in me that triggered them. Anyway, I wasn't ready for more tests. Maybe the pain would go away. Maybe when I was fit again.

Wincing, I bent over and lifted the bucket and staggered erratically down the long passage towards the kitchen. As I drew level with the front door there was a loud knock. Sighing, I lowered the bucket on to the floor and went to open the door. A young man dressed in blue overalls was standing outside.

'Good morning.'

'Morning, Ma'am,' he answered, doffing his cap. I waited.

'Errr, we're working next door.'

'Oh yes?'

'We're digging a hole for a swimming pool.'

'Oh.'

'Ma'am.'

'Yes?'

'At eleven o'clock there will be a loud noise.'

'Oh.'

'We just thought we'd tell you.'

'Thank you, that's very kind of you.'

'Bye Ma'am.'

'Bye,' I said, closing the door.

There had been loud noises coming from next door all morning. Why bother to inform me now? Judging by the sounds, they appeared to be drilling through solid rock, jackhammers going hell for leather. Shrugging, I lifted the bucket once more and carried it through the kitchen to the walled patio. I glanced at the clock on the kitchen wall as I went. It was a quarter to eleven. Nic was asleep in his cot and I hoped the loud noise wouldn't startle him. Whippy and Arrow wandered outside, watching as I began hanging nappies on the washline. When one line was full, I moved to the next. Suddenly there was the loud, shrill whoop of a siren.

'Don't worry, it's just the loud noise,' I told the dogs.

Then, without further warning, a tremendous explosion rent the air. The concrete under my feet heaved with the blast. Deafened, I gaped open-mouthed at the cloud of brown dust which mushroomed into the sky from next door. Whippy yelped once and shot indoors. Stunned, I glanced towards Arrow, who rose into the air and in one fluid leap, cleared the six-foot wall into the street.

'Arrow, ARROW!' I cried, running to the front door. Stumbling into the garden, I saw her racing madly up the middle of the road.

'Arrow . . . STOP!' I yelled. Paying no heed to my desperate cries, she hurtled on, oblivious to the traffic. Vehicles were hooting and swerving to avoid her.

'Oh dear God, don't let her be run over,' I prayed aloud, taking to the street after her. As I sprinted up the hill she disappeared over the rise. There was no way on earth that I could match her speed, she was built for running. Cresting the hill, gulping in air and almost in a state of collapse, I slowed to a walk. Then I spotted her. She was cringing against a garden hedge, eyes wild in her head, salivating profusely.

'Arrow,' I called softly as I approached her. She shivered fearfully, looking as if she might bolt any second.

'It's all right, it's over now,' I murmured soothingly. Crouching down, I reached out and began stroking her trembling body. After a few minutes I stood up and grasped her collar.

'Let's go home.'

As we neared the house she hung back, quaking with fear, and I was forced to pick her up and carry her inside. I closed her in our bedroom before rushing anxiously into Nic's room. He was still fast asleep with Whippy on the floor next to his cot.

'It must have been dynamite,' I told Dave indignantly that evening.

'Well, they did warn you.'

'He never said a word about dynamite, he merely mentioned a loud noise.'

'They're not likely to warn you about a siren.'

'How must I know that? Anything can happen in this godforsaken place,' I exclaimed bitterly.

A few days later Johannesburg became even more godforsaken, when I took Nic for his monthly check-up at the clinic.

'His head is too big,' said the young clinic sister, as she measured Nic's head.

'It looks fine to me.'

'It's too big in relation to his body.'

'My mother says everyone in our family was born with a big head. We grow into them.'

Her eyes flicked to my head. 'I'll check it again on his

next visit,' she murmured doubtfully.

I reflected on this conversation as I pushed the baby carriage towards home, the icy winter wind slicing through my clothes. It was not as if Nic had a huge lolling head on a tiny body, I thought grumpily. To me he appeared perfectly in proportion. I wished she would turn her attention elsewhere. One of the other babies had feet the size of skateboards. Now *that* definitely merited investigation.

'I'm not sure I can handle it,' I said to Dave.

'Handle what?'

'This clinic business.'

'Why?'

'I don't know. I just get the feeling that I can't cope with these clinic sisters.'

'But Chrystal, in what way?'

'Well, take today, for instance. The woman seems obsessed with the size of Nic's head. Do you think his head is too big?'

'No, his head is fine.'

'Well there you are then,' I said triumphantly, proving my point.

Dave sighed. 'Nic has to attend the clinic for his vaccinations.'

'Hmmmm.'

My attitude to clinics was beginning to resemble that of a dog contemplating a fight, hackles raised and circling warily.

A Peeping Tom

Holding the bottle up to the light, I checked that it was sparkling clean before reaching for another. Suddenly there was a dull *thunk* from the sitting-room and Splittie hurtled out into the passage and collided with the opposite wall. Bouncing off it and righting herself in a flurry of legs, she marched grimly down the passage towards our bedroom, every inch of her rigid body shrieking, '*Mortal offence!*'

'Splittie, what is it?' I called after her.

'*I've had it.*'

'Had what?'

'*He's just hit me with the gnome again. It's the third time today.*' She paused at our bedroom door, glaring back at me.

'I'm sorry, I'll speak to him.'

'*Huh.*'

As I watched, she disappeared into the bedroom stiff with disapproval. The words '*juvenile delinquent*' floated back to me.

Sighing, I continued with my task. There seemed to be a never-ending stream of dirty bottles and dirty nappies. As if they were breeding. Minutes later, there was another *thunk*, followed by a yelp, and Arrow slunk from the sitting-room, her tail between her legs.

I peeped around the doorframe. Nic, electric-blue eyes

sparkling, was vibrating excitedly in his little canvas chair. He had just lobbed a luminous-green rubber gnome across the room. As it landed, Whippy leapt up enthusiastically and trotted over to retrieve it. Grasping it once more in his sticky little hand, he hurled it into the air and the two of them followed it with their eyes, as it curved upwards in a parabola and then down, striking Mandy on the head. With a startled grunt, she sprang up and loped from the room looking annoyed.

Whippy had been promoted to Entertainment Director and she was doing an excellent job. Her first choice had been Catering Manager but, suspecting that her tasting tests would know no boundaries, I thought it wiser to fill that position myself.

Returning to the kitchen, I opened a bottle of puréed mutton and vegetables which had been warming in a jug of water. As I spooned the purée into Nic's mouth, Whippy eyed the level in the bottle anxiously. Finally, when Nic clamped his lips shut, refusing even one more spoonful, she sighed with relief. I offered her the rest. With the expertise born of experience, she probed the last smidgeon of purée from the corners, before turning her attention to Nic's face.

'Shall I clean his face?'

'I don't think so.'

'But there's so much food there, at least half a bottle.'

'Don't worry, I'll manage.'

'Are you sure?'

'Quite sure, thank you.'

Sighing wistfully, she retrieved the green gnome, placing it in Nic's hand once more. An Entertainment Director's work was never done.

'These cats justa won't stop scretching, Dottore,' exclaimed the client, lifting the cat carrier on to the consulting table. She was a dark-haired, attractive Italian woman, slightly excitable. Dave had first seen her a month before with her two itching cats.

He glanced at the card. 'Has there been any improvement since I saw them last?'

'Noh better, if anything, maybe worse, eh?'

'Did you change their diet as I recommended?'

'Yes I did it. I even killed the fleas as you suggest.'

'Hmmmm, when exactly did the scratching start?'

'It's been two month now and I worry, they scretching themselves raw.'

As Dave examined the two cats, running his hands over their fur, they twitched and scratched addictively.

'What about stress factors?'

'Whatta you mean, eh?'

'Have you moved house recently?'

'Noh.'

Has anything occurred in the past two months that would cause them stress?'

She looked thoughtful. 'Well, yes, now I think of eet,' she said. 'There is this big ginga cat. He start coming to our garden two month ago.'

'Does he fight with your cats?'

'Noh, noh, he does not fight. But they are scared of him, eh? When they see him come, they run. They run like mad.'

'You know, it is possible that the scratching is linked to this.'

'He sit outside on the kitchen window sill. He stare at them, he stare and stare. I phone the SPCA, eh? I say, "You come fetch this cat." They come, he not there. I'm worried Dottore, I'm worried they get sick from him. He always sneezing, always asneezing.'

As she uttered these words, Dave stiffened. He picked up her card and gazed at it in silence for a few seconds.

Embarrassed, he cleared his throat. 'Errr, Mrs Rosa.'

'Yes, Dottore?'

'Thatta . . .' stopping himself just in time '. . . That cat is not a stray.'

'But Dottore, how woulda you know, eh?'

'I think it may be our cat.'

'Scusi?'

'The cat belongs to us. I'm pretty sure it's our ginger cat. His name is Nuggie.'

She stared at him, confused.

'Look,' he said, pointing to the address on her card. 'You live one house away from us. We have a large ginger cat with chronic sinusitis who sneezes frequently.'

'Oh?' she said, taken aback.

'We moved into the house two months ago.'

They stared at each other for a few seconds and then both burst out laughing.

'You know, Dottore, that cat is eempossible, eempossible. When I pull down the blind, there is a small gap between blind and sill. He crouch down and put his eye to the gap.'

'I must apologise, Mrs Rosa, but don't worry, we'll sort it out.'

After she had left, Dave telephoned me. I listened to the story in stunned silence, wondering where Nuggie was at that moment. Replacing the receiver, I went out through the front garden and past our neighbour's house to the next house.

And there he was. Perched precariously on the window sill, bottom in the air, one eye glued firmly to the gap between blind and sill. Sherlock Holmes on the trail of something interesting.

'What do you think you're doing?' I hissed, sneaking up behind him.

Jerking guiltily, he almost fell off the sill.

'Come on, it's time to go home. The neighbours are complaining, eh?'

'*Complaining about what?*' he asked, looking embarrassed.

'About you, intimidating their cats.'

'*I'm just trying to make friends, only they never come outside.*'

'And they won't either, not while you're there.'

I took him home and poured him a saucer of milk. It occurred to me that it was fortunate he had not landed up at the SPCA. With his chronic sinusitis, he would've been taken for a stray with Snuffles and in all probability been euthanased.

As he drank the milk, my thoughts returned to the day when I had first seen him, a tiny ginger wisp of a kitten, covered in red ants.

Years before, I had been invited to a party at a farmhouse and in the kitchen I had noticed a cardboard box in a dark corner next to the fridge. Sitting up in the box watching me was an emaciated ginger cat. I strolled over to stroke her and peered into the box. There were three tiny ginger kittens crawling around inside, mewing piteously. The mother sat quietly as I picked one up in my hand. It seemed distressed and to my horror I saw that its fur was crawling with red ants. I examined the kitten more closely and found more red ants embedded in its flesh. I removed both mother and kittens from the box and lifted it. There was an ant nest underneath it. That was the end of the party as far as I was concerned. Taking them all with me, I left at once.

When I got home I went over them carefully and plucked off the ants. All three kittens had runny eyes and were sneezing at intervals. The mother cat was skin and bone and she gulped down the bowl of food I offered her. I wondered how on earth she could feed three kittens when she herself was in such a malnourished state. The next day I took them all to Dr Brown, a nearby vet. After vaccinating the mother, he dispensed antibiotics for the kittens. They had Snuffles, he told me.

Within days, despite the antibiotics, their condition deteriorated. They appeared to have difficulty breathing and when I took them back to Dr Brown, he diagnosed pneumonia. Three weeks of daily injections followed, as we battled to save them.

Finally, two of the kittens were pronounced healthy but the third continued to sneeze. I managed to find good homes for the mother and the two healthy kittens and decided to keep the third, the sneezing one.

'Call him Nugget,' my dad suggested cynically. 'After all the veterinary costs, he's worth his weight in gold.'

When Nugget was six months old, Dr Brown suggested that he operate to drain the sinuses, which had proved resistant to every antibiotic he had tried.

'It's a minor operation, with very few risks involved,' he told me.

After giving the matter some thought, I agreed. I loved Nuggie, he was a gentle, thoughtful cat.

On the day of the operation, I stopped in at the clinic on my way home from work. Nuggie was hunched miserably in a cage. When I spoke his name, he did not react at all. I opened the cage door to stroke him and found that his body was ice cold. He made no movement as I touched him, as if his mind was elsewhere.

'He looks quite bad,' I said to Dr Brown.

'Yes, he hasn't taken it very well and the operation took longer than expected.'

I stayed with him for a while. As I left, Dr Brown said he he was hopeful his condition would improve by the following day.

But there was no change the next afternoon. Nuggie remained crouched, with eyes closed and nose resting on the floor of the cage, as if he had withdrawn into pain and was waiting patiently to die.

'I'm taking him home,' I told Dr Brown.

'I strongly advise against it. His condition is serious and he requires medication.'

'I'll give him the medication at home. And I'll bring him back tomorrow evening for you to check. If he survives.' Reluctantly, Dr Brown agreed.

I put Nuggie in my bed, under the blankets and next to a hot-water bottle. Using a syringe, I force-fed him egg-flip.

'I'm sorry, but I'm not allowing you to die,' I told him firmly.

Later, after more egg-flip, I climbed under the blankets next to him. He raised his head and looked at me with dull eyes. I cuddled him throughout the night. At times his body would shudder as he moaned pathetically and I would stroke him gently until he was still. This happened several times, as if he was scared and needed comforting.

Early the next morning as I crept quietly from the bed he stirred and, opening his eyes, he stood up and stretched. I watched in amazement as he sprang down on to the floor and made his way unsteadily towards the litter tray.

That afternoon I took him back to Dr Brown who could not believe the change in him.

'What have you given him?' he asked, as Nuggie stood on the table, bright-eyed.

'Egg-flip,' I replied.

A few days later, he began coughing violently and refused solid food. Back we went to Dr Brown, who examined Nuggie's throat.

'There is no sign of inflammation,' he said.

But in the days that followed the coughing worsened. One morning, a week later, I watched anxiously as his whole body convulsed with coughing. I went to help him but he ran from me and as he ran I saw something protruding from his lips.

'Oh no, he's coughing up his insides,' I moaned, aghast.

As he ran, an object dropped on to the floor with a *clunk*. I picked it up and found myself gazing at an endotracheal tube. Printed on the side in white letters were the words 'Made in England'. Nuggie had spent two weeks with an endotracheal tube in his throat.

As he licked the last drop of milk from the saucer, I ran my hand along the fur on Nuggie's back and up his tail. I knew he was lonely, missing Philby, Carrots and Seafood. And missing the freedom of Swaziland, as we all were. That sensation of space. Space to breathe and run and shout and laugh.

Before I knew it another month had flown by and it was time for Nic to attend the clinic again. My heart sank when I entered the room to see the same young clinic sister as before. The clinic was held in a classroom at a local primary school in the afternoons when it was not in use. Mothers clasping babies sat behind small school desks, waiting their turn. There was absolutely no privacy. We could all hear every word the sister said as she dealt with each mother and child.

'This nappy rash looks septic,' she was saying sternly to one mother. 'What are you using on it?'

We all stared at the baby's bum, nodding amongst ourselves. It did look septic.

'Vicks,' the mother mumbled, looking embarrassed.

'VICKS!' the sister exclaimed in horror and the entire room looked shocked.

'I'm sorry, it was all I had,' the mother murmured abjectly, as we gazed on in disapproval.

Finally it was Nic's turn and I watched in silence as the sister weighed and examined him. Then, taking a tape measure from her pocket, she measured the length of his body and the circumference of his head.

'His head is still too big,' she said.

I glared at her. 'His head is fine,' I enunciated coldly.

'It's too big for his body.'

'If it was too big for his body, it would be lolling.'

'Mrs Sharp,' she said with an exasperated sigh, 'his body weight and length fall within the normal parameters for his age. His head exceeds those parameters.'

'By how much?' I asked, eyes narrowed.

'By four millimetres.'

'Four millimetres? Is that all?'

'Four millimetres is four millimetres,' she replied, speaking slowly as if I was mentally deficient.

'Look,' I said, speaking equally slowly, 'he is a perfectly happy normal baby. He eats, he drinks, he sleeps, he laughs, he's alert. He even poohs and wees.'

'That may be so, but we need to be sure. I'm referring him to the main clinic for further assessment. Anyway, he needs his next vaccination and they do that only at the main clinic in Germiston.'

Rolling my eyes heavenwards, I took the appointment card from her and we left.

I seethed all the way home.

Then I telephoned Dave at the practice.

'The clinic sister wants Nic assessed at the main clinic.'

'When?'

'Tomorrow afternoon.'

'What time?'

'Two-thirty.'

'All right, don't worry, I'll ask Dr Ward for the afternoon off.'

I wandered through to the bedroom where Nic was chortling happily in his little canvas chair, with Whippy in close attendance. Sitting down on the bed next to Splittie, I observed Nic thoughtfully. Everything about him was so normal, my instincts screamed out that there was nothing wrong.

'*Is something the matter?*' Whippy asked.

'Nic has to be assessed.'

'*Why?*'

'The clinic sister says his head is too big.'

'*But his head is perfect.*'

'Yes, I think so.'

'*Seafood's head was big when she was born,*' Splittie offered reassuringly. '*Do you remember?*'

'Yes.'

'*And there's nothing wrong with her.*'

'No.'

'*Except for her fascination with Philby,*' Splittie added, a cloud of worry settling on her brow.

The next afternoon, Dave collected Nic and me at two o'clock and we set off for the main clinic in Germiston.

'It's not as if they're peas in a pod,' I brooded.

'What do you mean?'

'Babies. They can't all be the same. They're individuals.'

'Of course they're individuals. No one expects them to be the same.'

'The clinic sister does.'

'She's young. She's most probably working strictly according to the book.'

'Well, I wish she'd read another book.'

The senior clinic sister referred Nic for X-rays – 'Just as a precaution,' she said. The paediatrician who examined the X-rays sent Nic for a CAT-scan.

'X-rays are useless,' he informed us.

The CAT-scan showed no abnormality.

Whippy was right. His head was perfect.

'We must leave this place.'

'Which place?'

'Johannesburg.'

'Where will we go?'

'Somewhere without a hospital. Or a clinic.'

'But, Chrystal, that doesn't make sense.'

'It does to me.'

Crossing the Line

Two and a half months later we left Johannesburg for the Eastern Cape. In those two and half months we managed to acquire a thirteen-year-old cat and a cockatiel named JP.

One morning Dave entered the consulting room to find two young men and a cat. The two young men were brothers and they said the cat had belonged to their mother who had passed away. She was thirteen years old and had been savaged by their young Rottweiler. (The cat, not the mother.) They wanted her euthanased. Dave could not find a mark on her, as she sat purring serenely on the table.

'But there is no sign of her having been savaged,' he said to the two young men.

'Well, if it hasn't happened yet, it will soon,' said the one, shrugging carelessly.

'The dog is becoming really vicious,' smirked the other.

'I see no need for this cat to be euthanased. She's perfectly healthy. Can't you find another home for her?'

'Look, Doctor, we don't want the cat. You can do with her what you like.'

They strode from the consulting room leaving Dave cuddling the cat on the table.

That evening I heard the bakkie pull into the garage and, walking through the kitchen door to the patio, I came face to face with Dave. He was carrying a cat carrier.

'What's in the cat carrier?'

'A cat.'

I nodded. Of course. Why had I asked?

'Whose cat?'

'Our new cat.'

Another stupid question.

We called her Fluffy. A Persian cross, her coat was mink-grey on the surface and a creamy white underneath.

She fitted into our lives with barely a ripple. The dogs accepted her as if she'd always been there. She was that kind of cat. Nuggie was thrilled to acquire an elderly aunt who licked him affectionately and spent hours listening to his reminiscences about Philby and Carrots and Swaziland. Even Splittie toed the line. Up to a point. Accepting that Fluffy was a *grande dame*, she treated her with respect. A grudging respect, but respect nevertheless. However, out of Fluffy's hearing she referred to her as 'the old bat'.

'Where is Nuggie?' I asked her one morning.

'In the garden with the old bat.'

'That's not a very nice thing to say.'

'Nice is not a word I care to dwell upon.'

Then Dave brought JP home. A dirty charcoal-grey, he was the ugliest cockatiel I had ever seen and miserable with it.

'He suffers from a recurring abscess above one eye. The owners are not prepared to persevere with treatment, so I said we'd take him.'

'He looks depressed.'

'If you had an abscess above your eye, you'd be depressed.'

'I suppose so. What does JP stand for?'

'I forgot to ask.'

Looking at the bird, who stared back at me apathetically, I suspected it was Jolly Pessimistic or something along those lines.

A few days later I asked, 'Aren't they supposed to sing?'

'What do you mean?'

'Cockatiels. Aren't they supposed to sing?'

Dave sighed heavily. 'I told you the bird is not well. I'm sure he'll sing when he's ready.'

I nodded diplomatically. To me it looked as if it had never sung in its entire life.

For some time the bakkie had been giving us trouble, and was in and out of the mechanic's workshop every two weeks or so. In desperation, we had bought an old battered canary-yellow Volkswagen Beetle to use while the bakkie was in for repairs. The mechanic who worked on the bakkie had taken to shaking his head gloomily when Dave enquired about the current problem.

'It's old, Doc, and tired. I won't be able to keep it on the road much longer.'

When we took the decision to leave Johannesburg, we realised that we would have to purchase a reliable vehicle. Finally, when the bakkie squatted stubbornly in the garage refusing to budge, we bought a Toyota Stallion. The Toyota dealer offered to tow the old bakkie away free of charge and, with tears in my eyes, I watched it being towed off down the street.

'Bye,' I whispered, waving forlornly.

Then I went inside and had a good cry.

We left Johannesburg at 7 o'clock on a Sunday evening. We would've left at 6.30 if Dave hadn't spent half an hour trying to find space for a 500 gram packet of honey-bush tea. Watching him move suitcases and boxes in an attempt to insert the packet of tea, I became increasingly desperate. At last, unable to stand it any longer, I urged: 'Dave, leave the tea.'

'But it's honey-bush tea.'

'The Eastern Cape is the home of honey-bush tea. We can buy more.'

Reluctantly he trailed over to our neighbours and presented them with the small packet as a parting gift.

I drove the Beetle. Nic dozed behind me in a baby carrier wedged securely on the rear seat. On the passenger seat next to me, JP perched in his cage covered by a large towel. Next to him, Splittie crouched on top of boxes which were crammed into the small floor area below the dashboard. We had decided to travel at night, hoping that Nic would sleep for the greater part of the journey. The animals, too, were always more restful at night.

Dave was behind the wheel of the new Toyota, with Nuggie and Fluffy in the front with him, while Mandy sat at his side like a queen surveying her loyal subjects. One could almost see the hand moving gently in a restrained wave to the crowds. In the canopied back area, Whippy and Arrow curled up on cushions surrounded by stacks of boxes and other paraphernalia. Both vehicles closely resembled sardine tins, with humans and animals only just slotting into their allocated places. There really wasn't room for that packet of tea.

Dave led the way and I followed. It was dusk when we set off from the house and darkness fell as we left the greater Johannesburg area. Storm clouds which had been brooding overhead chose that moment to split open and a deluge of rain and hail lashed down. A cloudburst of elemental fury.

Where is the switch for the windscreen wipers, I wondered, never having had occasion to use them before. As I fiddled and groped, trying to locate the switch, the headlights dimmed and went out. Ahead, I saw Dave's tail lights disappear into the distance.

'Oh no!' I moaned, in mounting panic.

I slowed down and pulled over to the left of the road. My heart thumping, I reached for the interior light switch above my head. It wasn't working. Jerking open the cubbyhole with desperate fingers, I scrabbled inside for a box of matches. Outside the night was as black as pitch and I had no idea whether or not we were still on the highway. Rain and hail smashed viciously against the roof and windscreen, filling the vehicle with their sound. Jiggling the headlight switch produced no result. Was there a loose connection somewhere?

'God, please help me,' I prayed aloud, hands shaking as I tried to light a match.

If another vehicle came speeding from behind and we were in its path, it would smash right into us. I could see nothing, absolutely nothing.

The match flared and as it flickered and went out, I peered at the dashboard. I lit a second match, praying all the while. Suddenly, the interior of the Beetle was flooded with bright light. To my horror, I saw in the rear-view mirror a pair of headlights approaching like a steamtrain. In that split second of icy fear when I could not move, they swerved, avoiding us, and roared past with hooter blaring. I pulled at the headlight switch again and light beamed out on to the tar. Almost crying with relief, I found the windscreen wiper button and the wipers began sweeping across the glass.

I pulled off slowly into the night, wondering where Dave was now. Had he noticed that we were no longer behind him or was he hurtling on, oblivious to our absence? Even if he had noticed, he would not have been able to turn back on the motorway to look for us. Approximately two kilometres further on, I saw the Toyota parked at the side of the road with Dave standing next to it, gazing back anxiously in our direction. I pulled in behind the Toyota and told him what had happened.

'I think I should travel in front now,' I said, 'in case the headlights fail again.'

The kilometres slipped by in the darkness. Twice we stopped to fill up with petrol and exercise the animals. Nic slept. In the early hours of the morning, as dawn seeped into the sky, I knew we were close.

A while later, as we drove slowly down a mountain pass, the first rays of sunlight touched the landscape, intensifying the shadows. To my right the ground fell away into a gorge far below, before sweeping upwards into majestic hills. The hills bordered a valley – The Valley of Desolation, it was called, but for me the valley of desolation lay hours behind, in that place of gold.

Somewhere between Philippolis and Colesberg we crossed the invisible line into the Eastern Cape. Here the air was crisp and clean. The hills God made were bathed in the pale luminous light of dawn, a welcome contrast to the man-made hills of Johannesburg, the mine-dumps – symbols of man's ability to take from the earth, leaving ugliness behind. These hills were pristine, untouched. Suspended in the ice-blue sky, I saw a jackal buzzard scanning the scrubland for prey. It was the start of a new day.

A feeling of freedom surged up from my toes and I laughed out loud. Just for the joy of it. Splittie opened one eye and gave me a bleary look before closing it again. Just after ten o'clock we pulled into my mother's driveway. The hibiscus trees which had been chest high when I last saw them towered above our heads, heavily laden with red and pink blooms. The hedge surrounding the property tumbled over the wire fence in a profusion of orange flowers. Everywhere I looked there was colour and for the first time I realised that it was spring.

I found Philby in the back garden squatting on a rock, studying a lizard.

'Philby,' I called.

His head jerked around and he stared at me in disbelief. *'What are you doing here?'*

'Didn't Granny Fay tell you we were coming?'

'Yes, but Carrots didn't believe her. He said we mustn't raise our hopes, only to have them dashed.'

'Strange, Carrots is not usually that cynical.'

'Hmmmm,' his eyes shifted back to the lizard.

I sat down on the grass next to him and stroked his fur.

'It's been pretty boring here.'

'I'm sorry.'

'Except for the time the tanks came.'

'What tanks?'

'Oh, there was a war or something,' he shrugged. *'They were shooting teargas and rubber bullets.'*

'Why?'

'I don't know. And Granny Fay gave me a hiding.'

'What for?'

'I don't know. All I did was sit on the pavement and watch the tanks.'

Suddenly Carrots was at my side, rubbing his face against my legs.

'*I told Philby you were coming,*' he purred happily.

'*Look, there's Seafood,*' said Philby, changing the subject.

I glanced up to see Seafood's face peering at me from amongst the leaves of the fig tree.

'Seafood,' I called out.

At that precise moment a stentorian voice bellowed out from behind me: '*Seafood, COME!*'

I turned to see Splittie standing on the kitchen steps. As quickly as it had appeared, Seafood's face disappeared amongst the leaves.

I smiled. Nothing had changed.

That evening when my mother returned from work she rushed into the house, pausing only briefly to give Dave and me a peck on the cheek.

'Where's Nicholas?'

'In the cot in our bedroom.'

She disappeared into the bedroom, emerging a moment later with Nic in her arms.

'He's beautiful,' she whispered, tears rolling down her cheeks. Toys were produced from every corner of the house. When Nic laughed, my mother laughed and then he laughed because she was laughing. It just went on and on.

Two hours later, I tried for the third time to broach the subject of the teargas and the rubber bullets.

'What's this I hear about teargas and rubber bullets?'

'What?'

'Philby mentioned teargas and rubber bullets.'

'Oh that. Look at this one, Nic. See, if you shake it a bell rings inside.'

'Mom?'

'Yes?'

'What happened?'

'No, don't put that in your mouth, it's dirty.'

'MOM!'

Finally, I managed to drag the story from her.

Across the road from her house there was a large field and where the field ended, a squatter camp began. The local authority had decided that the squatters must be relocated to another area, where housing and sanitation had been provided. The squatters refused to move as most of them were employed in the area. The police were ordered to forcibly evict them. They resisted, tempers flared, police vehicles were stoned and petrol bombed and the army was called in.

'When I came home that evening, there were two tanks in the road and an overturned police van was burning in the field. I rushed inside to check if all the animals were safe. They were all here, except Philby.'

Dave and I nodded cynically.

'So then I ran out into the road and around the corner and there he was. Sitting on the pavement in the middle of a running battle between squatters and soldiers. One of the soldiers waved me back, but I pointed to Philby and shouted that I needed to get my cat. He shook his head and as I picked Philby up, the first teargas canisters exploded. There were bullets whizzing through the air and by the time we entered the house, our eyes were streaming from the teargas.'

'What did you do?'

'I bathed mine with milk, but when I tried to do Philby's he kept kicking and wriggling and all the milk went into his ears. In the end I gave him a hiding.'

'Mom, I'm really sorry.'

'Chrystal, are you sure Philby is an ordinary cat?'

'He is a bit of a handful,' I said and noticed Dave staring at me with his mouth hanging open.

'He's more than that. Much more.'

A Sea Change

When we decided to leave Johannesburg, we had considered various options. Returning to Swaziland was out of the question. The arrangement with the Swazi vet, whereby we worked for a percentage of the professional fees, had not been financially viable. As a South African citizen, Dave would not be permitted to open his own practice there.

In the end we decided to open a practice in the small coastal town where Dave's parents lived.

There is something about the Eastern Cape. It allows you to leave for a while and then one day, it says 'COME'.

And you go.

Dolphin Bay had approximately five thousand permanent residents. Opening a veterinary practice there might be a risky venture, but we decided to try anyway. Hilary and Andries, friends of Dave's parents, had recently erected a double-storey building. It had two apartments on the top floor and four offices/shops below. One of the office suites would be perfect for veterinary consulting rooms, they said.

We spent a few days with my mother before setting off for Dolphin Bay. Initially we would be living with Dodo and Bill, but just until we could find a suitable house to rent. Because of this, we considered leaving Philby, Carrots and Seafood with my mother until we had our own accommodation. After all, they seemed settled and quite happy.

'*We're not settled, we're bored,*' Philby stated flatly, when I mentioned this plan to him.

'It would only be for a few weeks.'

'*Carrots says that if he has to stay here FOR ONE MORE DAY, he'll sicken and die. From boredom.*'

'Funny, Carrots never mentioned anything to me.'

'*Well, you know Carrots.*'

'I certainly do.'

My mother threw her support behind Philby. 'He's right, you must take them with you,' she said, a note of desperation in her voice.

So we took them all with us. Leaving the Beetle behind for the headlights to be checked, we loaded the bakkie with people, animals and clothing. The Beetle and the rest of our possessions would have to be collected later.

It was late afternoon by the time we set off and one hour later, as we rounded the hill above the Fish River, we saw the sea in the distance.

'*WOW!*' breathed Philby, as he and Carrots leaned on the dashboard and stared at the huge expanse of water.

At my feet, Splittie was lecturing Seafood on the dangers of bluebottles and riptides and I heard Philby whisper something to Carrots. Something about sharks.

'THERE WILL BE NO SHARKS,' I said firmly.

The sun was setting behind the surrounding hills as we crossed the narrow bridge over the Tunny River. Its dying rays scalloped the clouds with a flamboyant pink-golden glow. As we approached the turn-off to Dolphin Bay, the Tunny lagoon lay below us on our left. Not a ripple disturbed the surface, a mirror reflection of bush and radiant sky. The only crack in the glass came from a huge tree trunk, remnant of a flood, crouched in its centre. On the twisted salt-blackened branches two fish eagles perched. Lords of the lagoon. Raptor eyes watched as we turned off the main road and slowed, pulling to the side. Opening the windows we breathed in the rich salty air, tasting it in our mouths. As we sat quietly drinking in the scene, one of the eagles spread its wings and in a lazy slow motion, lifted itself from the trunk, spiralling up into the sky. Up and up it went and suddenly, from high in the heavens above us, we heard its haunting cry. We savoured the greeting in silence. Then the spell was broken as Dave switched on the ignition and we travelled the last few kilometres to his parents' home.

Dodo and Bill lived in a dark-red facebrick house on a circular dirt road. In the centre of the circle was a dam bordered by thick reeds and water grass. From its banks knee-high grass and veld flowers extended to the road. As the bakkie drew to a halt opposite their front door we heard the sound of frogs. Choirs of them, announcing the night.

Coming from the arms of one fan club into the arms of another, Nic was in his element. But before long his eyelids were drooping and we laid him down in the cot they had prepared. All in all, it had been a long day.

After supper Dave and I drifted outside, absorbing the stillness and the night sky strewn with stars.

'Let's walk down to the dam,' I suggested. As we strolled along the driveway and crossed the gravel road, Philby popped out from a bush, closely followed by Carrots, Seafood and Nuggie. Then Splittie was there, marching at our sides. And Fluffy. The dogs raced on ahead. As I stood quietly in the long grass gazing at the silvery water, I felt Philby brush against my legs.

'*We're a family again,*' he whispered, eyes gleaming in the moonlight.

'Yes.'

Over the next few weeks we concentrated on getting the surgery up and running. Dave made a few trips to the nearest city to collect surgical equipment and the range of drugs he considered essential.

Up to our eyeballs in debt, we opened our doors. From day one, Dodo and Bill's circle of friends trotted their animals in and out, for check-ups and vaccinations.

At the end of December we found a house to rent on the seafront. The only snag was that we would have to vacate the house every December, when the owners used it themselves. This problem paled into insignificance at the thought of living so close to the sea and we moved in on the fifteenth of January.

It was in the nick of time, as Bill's mutters regarding the manner in which I sliced bread were becoming increasingly vehement.

'You must leave a straight edge,' he'd growl impatiently.

'I'm trying, I'm trying,' I'd reply, feeling harassed.

The house was old and weather-beaten and squatted like a benevolent gnome in a slight hollow overlooking the sea. Directly behind it, bordering the dirt road, lay a vacant plot of uneven humps covered in grass and indigenous shrubs. Along one side of the plot a driveway extended from the road to the house. The exterior walls of the house were plastered in unpainted cement and rough pebbles. There were three bedrooms, a large sitting-room, a dining-room, kitchen, bathroom and separate toilet. The kitchen, dining-room and Nic's bedroom were on the side facing the plot, while our bedroom, the sitting-room and the spare bedroom faced the sea.

The walls of the sitting-room, like the exterior walls, were

233

plastered in cement and pebbles and it lacked a ceiling – one looked up at the wooden beams supporting the roof. Somehow this gave an impression of airy spaciousness.

The garden was lush with a mixture of indigenous and exotic trees and plants. A huge pawpaw tree, tumbles of bougainvillaea, an old tree aloe, beds of bulbs, irises, daffodils, clumps of violets and impatiens were scattered around. After the sterile garden in Johannesburg, it was a feast of colour and smells. In the front garden facing the sea bromeliads and ferns flourished under a thicket of wind-blown milkwood trees. From the sitting-room, French windows opened on to an area of mossy lawn which extended to the dunes at the edge of the property. The dunes were decked in thick, waist-high indigenous bush and a small stone pathway wound down through the bush to the beach below.

The house was filled with the sound of the sea. It sang through the rooms, sometimes a hushed whisper stroking the mind and spirit, at other times a roaring crescendo of elemental noise reverberating against roof and walls. As the days passed, I often found myself sharing its moods. When it was calm and still I reflected the hush inside of me. On stormy days I would feel jumpy and restless, unable to settle.

One morning a few weeks after we had moved in, I took a watering-can out on to the veranda where a small rockery nestled in one corner. Carrots was sitting on the steps leading down into the garden. When he saw me he jumped up and came over, purring loudly.

'Where's Philby?' I asked casually.

'*Down there,*' he indicated the bushes at the foot of the steps. He looked slightly shifty. I gazed at him thoughtfully, then turned away and began watering the plants.

As the last drop of water dripped from the can, I swung

round to return to the house. I stopped, surprised. Carrots and Philby and a cat I had never seen before were sitting in a row watching me.

'Hello,' I exclaimed.

'*This is our new friend,*' explained Carrots.

'*He's just come out of the infirmatory,*' Philby added, eyes sparkling.

'Infirmary,' I corrected.

'*He said infirmatory.*'

I looked at the cat.

'*Reformatory,*' he mumbled, looking sheepish.

I stared at him. He was a large silver and black tabby, his body big-boned but thin with the rangy look of an uncastrated male.

'*He says he's hungry,*' Carrots offered. '*And he doesn't have a home.*'

'Oh.'

'*Philby said he could come and live with us.*'

'Oh yes?'

Without more ado, Silverkitty moved in. Two weeks later, when his general condition had improved, Dave took him into the surgery one morning and castrated him. Much to Splittie's disgust. From the start she flirted outrageously with him, mincing along daintily on her crippled legs and tossing her head like a Bournemouth Beauty when he was watching.

He settled in quickly and he, Philby, Carrots and Nuggie would slink off together into the bush-covered dunes on hunting expeditions. Seafood would accompany them if she managed to evade Splittie's watchful eye for long enough.

'What are you hunting? Buck?' I asked Philby one day.

'*No, leopard.*'

I smiled cynically. 'This isn't Swaziland, my boy. There are no leopards here.'

Green sparks glinted in his eyes as he looked away. Later, we discovered that there were in fact two leopards living in the dunefields.

You had to hand it to that cat. He knew his leopards.

Late one afternoon there was a knock on the front door and I opened it to find two policemen standing on the veranda.

'Mrs Sharp?'

'Yes?'

'Is Doctor here? We have a sick seabird in the van.'

'I'm sorry, he's out on a farm call.'

They looked at each other. 'We don't know what to do with the bird.'

'Well, I could put it in the patio until he gets back.'

They looked relieved. I walked with them to the van and watched as they opened the two rear doors. Crouched on the floor of the van was a magnificent bird. Large, the size of a well-fed duck, it was white with touches of black on the wings. The head was a delicate yellow and a black line ran along the edge of the beak, encircling the powder-blue eyes, as if it was wearing make-up. The blue-grey beak was long and pointed.

The two policemen stood back and watched me expectantly. Slightly surprised, I realised that they were waiting for me to remove the bird.

'What kind of bird is it?' I asked.

'We think it's a gannet. It bites,' said one, holding up his hand for me to see. Blood was seeping from a deep gash across his palm. I regarded the gash speculatively for a moment and then, girding my loins, reached forward into the van. Maybe if I lifted it keeping the head facing away from me, it wouldn't be able to bite.

Gently sliding my hands under its body, I gripped it firmly and stepped back, holding it at arm's length. In that split second there was a lightning flash of movement as the head whipped around 180 degrees and the beak slashed across my throat.

'AARRGH!' I screamed.

One of the policemen sprang to the rescue. Gripping the bird's head in his hand, he immobilised the razor-sharp beak.

'Why didn't you do that in the first place?' I glared at him.

'Sorry lady, we thought you knew how to handle these birds,' he said, looking embarrassed.

'If I knew how to handle it, I wouldn't have asked what kind of bird it was, would I?' I retorted angrily, blood pouring down my neck and soaking my T-shirt.

That evening when Dave returned from the farm I informed him that there was a gannet in the patio area.

'What's that on your neck? he asked curiously.

'A bandage.'

'Is the gannet sick or injured?'

'I don't know.'

'Didn't you examine it?'

'No.'

'Will you give me a hand with it now?'

'I'm sorry, I'm busy. Ask Johannes.'

Shortly after we moved into the house, Dave had employed Johannes to assist him in the surgery and accompany him on farm calls. They had worked together previously at a practice where Dave had been doing a locum. The practice had since changed hands and Johannes had been retrenched.

Johannes was of Khoisan ancestry. His head appeared slightly too large for his thin wiry body and he had big brown eyes and a ready smile, if at times somewhat sardonic. Fortunately the house had an extra room outside, plus a shower and toilet. Johannes moved into this room and early every morning he and Dave would set off for the surgery, returning at lunchtime if there were no farm calls.

The surgery was housed in a corner suite of rooms on the ground floor of the double-storeyed building. It consisted of a large waiting area, a small office, a theatre-cum-consulting room, a small storage area and a toilet. Fortunately the consulting room-cum-theatre was spacious enough to accommodate several loose cages, ranging in size from small to very big.

'Johannes is off for the weekend,' Dave said one Saturday afternoon, 'and I might need some help with a bird that's in hospital.'

'That's fine. Nic can play in the waiting-room while we're busy.'

When we got to the surgery I deposited Nic on the carpeted floor with a selection of toys and followed Dave into the consulting room. I closed the door behind me.

'Where's the bird?' I asked, looking around. There was not a parrot cage in sight.

'In here,' he said, squatting down before the largest of the cages.

'What kind of bird is it?' I asked, puzzled by the size of the cage.

Without bothering to reply, Dave slid the bolt back and the cage door swung open. There was a loud *thump* as a hulking great black and white bird waddled out into the room.

In one fluid movement, Dave leapt behind the cage and

the bird lurched towards me, spreading its enormous wings as it charged. I hesitated, wondering whether its intentions were honourable.

'RUN!' Dave shouted.

'WHERE TO?' I shrieked, breaking into a trot around the consulting table with the bird hot on my heels.

'THE DESK! Get up on the desk.'

As it launched itself at me, I sprang up on to the desk and huddled there, heart racing.

'What is it?'

'An albatross.'

'My God, it's huge.'

A fisherman had brought the unconscious bird in that morning. Dave had been unable to find any injury.

'It looks fine now,' I observed succinctly, from atop the desk.

'It must have been stunned, maybe from a blow to the head.'

'What are we going to do?'

'We'll have to get it back into the cage somehow. I'll ask the fisherman to help me release it tomorrow.'

It took a long time to get that bird back into the cage. Armed with brooms and using wastepaper bins as shields, we attempted to manoeuvre it in the direction of the cage. Dave informed me that the local sailors called them 'Cape sheep'.

'They're not very easy to herd.'

'It must be a reference to their size.'

'Ah.'

Early the next morning I watched from a safe distance as it took off from the sand, flying low above the misty waves, heading straight out into the bay. Albatross are deep sea birds and to view one from close up was a privilege, Dave

told me. A bit of a mixed privilege I thought, a bit too close
up.

 # What's in a Penguin?

'What is it?' I asked the youngster, staring at the bedraggled bundle of feathers clasped proudly in his hands.

'I don't know, Ma'am, I found it lying on the beach.'

'It's a tern,' Dave said coming up behind me.

'Oh.'

As one week melted into the next and gloriously sunny days piled up, one after the other, the words, 'What is it?' seemed to become embedded in my vocabulary.

In the early days at the coast my knowledge of marine birds was limited to being able to identify a seagull. At close range. But as the weeks passed, I learned that they all had one thing in common. Without exception, they were all capable of inflicting a painful bite. The beaks varied in size, shape and colour, as did the bite-wounds. The smaller species seemed to make up for their lack of size by hanging on grimly to whatever part of your anatomy they could reach. It often required two people to prise the beak apart. The larger birds wielded their beaks like swords and a momentary lack of concentration could result in a very painful wound.

'What is it?' I asked yet again one Sunday morning, looking into the small cardboard box which Dave had just deposited on the sitting-room carpet.

'It's a penguin.'

'What's the matter with it?'

'I'm not sure. I think it's a baby, it may just be weak.'

The penguin was lying on its stomach, unmoving. I bent down cautiously to touch it and discovered that it was ice cold.

'It's very cold. Shall I make it a hot-water bottle?'

'Yes, but not too hot.'

Five minutes later I returned with the hottie wrapped in an old towel. I lifted the small body and placed the hottie underneath it. The penguin had its eyes closed and was barely breathing. Dave injected an antibiotic and vitamins and ran a drip in under the skin of the neck. Two hours later it stopped breathing.

Its little body lay limp in Dave's hands as he examined it curiously. Neither of us had ever been this close to a penguin before. They were something we'd encountered on television or in books, never on the sitting-room carpet.

Its feathers were soft and sleek and packed tightly for insulation. From the throat to the lower abdomen, they were white with stipples of black. The head and the rest of the body was charcoal-grey, with a blue sheen to it. The feathers ended halfway down the legs and the remainder of the legs and webbed feet were encased in a leathery black-grey skin.

I noticed that each of the three toe digits ended in a small curved nail and on the side of each foot was a dewclaw, similar to those found in dogs and cats. The two flippers resembled blunt, slightly curved boomerangs and they extended from its shoulders almost to its feet. They were covered in small hard feathers which looked as if they were glued to the skin.

'Look, this must be its oil gland,' Dave said, parting the feathers just above the tail. Its beak was long, fairly narrow, with a nostril on either side of the upper half and when Dave opened it, we could see the mucous membranes were very pale, almost white.

'It was obviously very anaemic.'

'Why would that be?'

'I'm not sure. It could be shock or internal parasites . . . worms,' he added for my benefit.

Sadly, and wishing we had been able to do more for it, we placed it in a black bag for disposal.

This was our first penguin. But not our last.

A few days after this, at the age of fourteen months, Nic started running. I've often wondered if there was any connection.

When we first arrived in Dolphin Bay, Dodo and Bill had expressed concern that Nic showed no inclination to walk. Dodo went out and bought a bright blue walking-ring. Although she never admitted it, I think she had reason to regret this purchase. He operated the ring as a military man would a tank. Ominous dull rumbles would announce its approach as it trundled through rooms, thudding against family heirlooms, walls and doors. When confronted by a chair or table, the walking-ring would simply proceed to mount the obstacle, only to tumble back defeated. Frustrated wails would bring us rushing into a room to find Nic on his back, still in the ring, floundering like an upside-down turtle.

One evening, as Dave and I were chatting in the sitting-room, Nic crawled to the chair beside me. As I glanced at him, he grunted once, hauled himself up on to his feet, turned, took a deep breath and hurtled the full length of the room. It was a very long room. When he reached the far wall he promptly fell over. We stared in stunned silence as he pulled himself up against the wall and ran back to us, laughing gleefully. Mesmerised, we watched him flash by, first one way, then the other.

Eventually, rousing myself as from a deep slumber, I said, 'Dave, phone your Mom and Dad.'

In one fell swoop, Nic had progressed from crawling to running. In his scheme of things, walking was not a prerequisite.

It wasn't long before the implications of this new development sank in and I entered a new phase of motherhood. The one where you grow eyes in the back of your head.

I was washing dishes at the kitchen sink a few days later when I noticed that the house seemed unnaturally quiet. I went through to the sitting-room where Nic had been thumping wooden blocks a few minutes before, and I found it deserted. No Nic, no dogs, no cats. Puzzled, I checked the other rooms. Nothing. The front lawn was devoid of any sign of life. Heart racing, I rushed through the dining-room and out on to the veranda. Pausing, I listened for any sound that would indicate his whereabouts but there was only silence. Which direction should I search first, I wondered? The sea or the road?

'THE SEA!' screamed my mind, imagination kicking in with a picture of mountainous waves tumbling in towards a very small boy.

Feet barely touching the ground, I hurtled down the path and the seven cats huddled at the bottom scattered as I burst through them on to the sand. A maternal missile.

And then I saw him. Fifty metres away to my right, Nic was standing on a shelf of rocks surrounded on three sides by a boiling churning sea. He was trying to move forward towards the crashing waves but was blocked by Mandy, who had planted herself firmly in his path. Whippy and Arrow were pressed against his sides, Whippy gazing back anxiously in my direction.

Flying across the sand in a cold sweat of fear, I noticed a group of people further down the beach. They were pointing at Nic and the dogs, obviously concerned at the sight of such a young child on the rocks. The tide was pushing in strongly. Stumbling over the rocks, I scooped him into my arms. Whippy's worried look was transformed into one of sheer relief.

Nic protested loudly as I stomped across the sand towards the path.

'Never, ever, do that again,' I told him severely. 'You are never, ever, to go to the beach on your own again.' He glared at me mutinously through his tears.

Once inside the house, I dumped him unceremoniously on the sitting-room carpet and closed and locked the French windows. Striding through to the kitchen, I switched the kettle on. If there was ever a need for a strong cup of tea, it was then.

I left Nic ill-temperedly bashing blocks together, still looking defiant, and nipped into the bathroom to remove the load of washing from the machine. Two minutes later, carrying the basket of wet clothing, I re-entered the sitting-room and stopped dead. The room was empty. No Nic, no dogs, no cats. Dropping the basket on the floor, I flung open the French windows and raced out and down the path to the beach. This time the beach was deserted. I sprinted madly back up the path into the house and checked all the rooms. In the dining-room I found the door to the veranda standing open.

'Oh no, the road,' I moaned.

Barefooted, ignoring the thorns, I shot through the

garden, down the driveway and on to the gravel road.

Seven cats were sitting in a group on the plot, gazing interestedly in the direction of a nearby field. I raced down the road and as I passed the last house I saw him. With Mandy on one side, Whippy on the other and Arrow bringing up the rear, Nic was running across the field towards me. I stopped, breathless, and watched their approach. The dogs had placed themselves so strategically that the only direction in which he could move was towards home. They were herding him back to me.

One sad day JP came to an untimely end. When Silverkitty took up residence with us, we decided that JP would have to go and live at the surgery. Philby, Carrots and the gang had shown no interest in him whatsoever. Bedraggled specimen that he was, I suspected that they did not recognise him as a member of the avian family. Silverkitty was different. He would gaze at JP with a secret gleam in his eyes. He was used to potluck.

So JP moved to the surgery. He was happy there in his cage on a table in the waiting-room, where he received lots of sunlight and sympathy.

'Oh shame, poor little thing,' clients would exclaim. 'What is it?'

'A cockatiel,' Dave would reply with an icy glare.

'Oh really?'

One of the clients, a lawyer named Hennie Smith, owned an extremely overweight dachshund named Canis.

'Hennie, this dog will have to lose weight,' Dave told him. 'His back problem is going to become progressively worse if he doesn't.'

'I know, Doc, I know, but my wife is always feeding him titbits at home. She says he looks at her with those big brown eyes and she can't say no.'

'Well in that case, I'll have to hospitalise him. I'm going to put him on the Nil Diet.'

At the time the Nil Diet was used in cases of severe overweight in dogs. It involved a regime of fluids and vitamin supplements for three to six weeks. No solid food at all.

Two weeks into his Nil Diet, Canis ate JP.

Johannes had removed the tray base from JP's cage that morning in order to clean it. When he locked up at lunchtime he forgot to replace the tray. Canis was allowed to roam the surgery when it was closed. To encourage exercise.

When Dave returned from a house-call shortly after-wards, all that remained of JP were a few charcoal-grey feathers on the waiting-room floor. Furious with Johannes and furious with Canis, Dave telephoned Hennie's wife and asked her to come and fetch the dog.

'You can continue with the Nil Diet at home,' he told her coldly.

That afternoon Hennie phoned Dave at the surgery, puzzled as to the reason for Canis' discharge.

'I've weighed him, he's only lost a half a kilogram, Doc.'

'Well, what do you expect?' Dave burst out bitterly. 'He ate our cockatiel.'

We were horrified at the nature of JP's demise.

'But,' as I said to Dave that evening, 'it's almost as though his personality required such an ending.' A tragic life, a tragic death.

I patted Dave on the shoulder as he mumbled something about 'Not even being able to give him a decent burial.'

A Second Path

After our initial contact with a penguin, we had made
enquiries in town, only to discover that penguins on the
beaches in the area were not such a rare occurrence after all.
We discovered that our landlady Hilary had nursed quite a
few penguins back to health and she introduced us to Ruth
and Jenny, who had been rehabilitating individual birds on
and off over the years. They informed us that at fairly regular
intervals, penguins who were sick or injured made their way
into the bay. The islands which were their main breeding
grounds were situated about 120 kilometres east of Dolphin
Bay.

Our second encounter with the species was in the plural,
not the singular.

During a spell of stormy weather, a ship ran aground on
the rocks just west of Dolphin Bay. As it lay on the rocks
battered by heavy seas, oil spewed from its tanks into the
surrounding ocean. Within days heavily oiled penguins were
being brought in to the surgery by concerned members of
the public. This became a learning experience for us.

As they were brought in, some already in a state of
collapse, we placed them in open cardboard boxes and crates.
Initially they had to be force-fed twice daily. After a few
days, still in boxes and crates, they began taking fish from

our hands. There were thirty-six penguins in all and before long the facilities at the surgery were being strained to their limits. Once they had been stabilised, they needed to be washed and we decided to transfer the boxes and crates to the enclosed patio off the kitchen at the house, where there was more space for the washing process.

The night sky was sprinkled with stars and in the east a full moon loomed over the sea. Like a giant torch it cast a beam of moonlight across the shimmering waters straight towards the house. A lunar pathway to our door.

Dave appeared at my side. 'Chrystal, will you feed the penguins tomorrow?'

'What?' I gazed at him, shaken from my reverie.

'The penguins, will you feed them tomorrow?'

'Me? On my own?'

'Yes. Johannes and I have a farm call at 7.30, we won't have the time to feed them before we leave.'

'If you think I can manage.'

'We've let them loose in the patio.'

'Oh.' It occurred to me that this could develop into more than a learning experience.

'If you think you won't manage, leave it and we'll feed them when we get back.'

'No, it's all right. I'll do it.' I stared at him with narrowed eyes.

As the door swung open, the group of baby penguins who had been leaning against it tumbled head-over-heels into the kitchen.

'Oh bugger!' I exclaimed as their little feet left imprints in faeces on the tiles. Clustering around me they began pecking hopefully at my wellies.

'*I told you not to open it*,' said Philby smugly, from his safe position on the kitchen dresser.

Ignoring him, I tried to nudge the little bodies out of the door but they kept bouncing back, as if attached to my feet by elastic strands. Fearful of treading on them, I waded gingerly through, with a bucket of fish in one hand and a barbecue grid in the other.

As I descended the steps into the brick-paved patio they followed closely on my heels. Reaching back to pull the door closed behind me, I glimpsed Philby's face peering down, round-eyed. He had donned his '*Something interesting is going to happen*' look.

'I could do with some assistance here,' I called to him. Suddenly engrossed in a moth on the wall, he appeared not to hear.

Wild and terrified, the oil-soaked adults huddled in corners, while the babies gathered around me hungrily. Wielding the grid to separate individuals from the crowd, I plunged my hand into the bucket and began to feed them. As the babies ate, the adults approached nervously, ready to flee at any sudden movement. Using 'hit-and-run' tactics, they dived savagely at the fish in my hand, running off while still in the act of swallowing. Unfortunately, 'hit-and-run' vied with 'hit-and-miss', as my bare knees and arms became targets.

As the last fish was ripped from my grasp, I turned and raced up the steps, with a few diehards at my heels.

'There is no more fish,' I said firmly, shutting the door before they came in to check for themselves.

I staggered to a chair and dissolved into it, aware that I had fish slivers splattered liberally across my face, spectacles, arms and legs. Blood dripped from several nasty slashes on my hands and knees, bearing witness to their attempts to eat anything that moved. Be it fish or flesh. As I tried to stem the blood with streams of toilet paper, I wondered if penguins were short-sighted.

'It's a fish-bath out there,' I muttered to Philby, who was still sitting on the dresser, watching me speculatively.

Our eyes met and locked as I waited for him to comment. Poker-faced, his eyes slid away from mine, then flicked back filled with glee. The swine. He was the only cat I knew who could laugh with a straight face. Suddenly distracted by a strange tickling sensation in my nose, I discovered a fish scale on its way up my right nostril. I sneezed violently and it flew out. As I sniffed the smell of pilchards which hung over me like an aura became unbearable.

'Come on,' I said to Philby. 'Let's go down to the beach.'

As we strolled through the sitting-room, the other six cats who were sprawled on the settee jumped down and tagged along behind. Outside on the lawn, Mandy, Whippy and Arrow leapt up, following me enthusiastically down the narrow winding path.

The silky sand was devoid of all footprints except our own. Standing knee-deep in the sparkling blue water I rinsed my arms and legs, splashing water on to my face and breathing in the salty smell. In the lazy blue sky above seagulls floated in slow motion, their clattering calls filtering downwards. In the distance, through a shimmering haze of sun reflecting off rocks and water, I saw Ruth stooping over searching for sole, sunlight sparking off her metal trident.

Spread-eagled against a sun-warmed dune, I watched as the dogs cavorted on the sand. The cats rubbed against me, then rolled on their backs slowly from side to side, soaking up the heat. Filling my palm with sand and letting it trickle through my fingers, I pondered the uniqueness of life. I wondered if anyone else in the world had fed thirty-six oiled penguins after breakfast today? Or was I the only one?

I lay back, lulled by the sunlight and the muffled swish of waves whispering ancient secrets as they broke. Digging my toes into the warm sand, my mind wafted, floating on high with the seagulls. These were halcyon days, I thought contentedly.

But even halcyon days can be disturbed.

A few weeks later two significant events occurred.

After dark one evening, I ambled down the path on to the sand and settled back comfortably against my favourite dune. The weather had been overcast all day and there was not a single star to be seen. Quietly stroking Philby and Carrots, I sat in contemplative silence. Although the sky was stormy, the sea was fairly still. Suddenly we heard a deep unearthly sound. It seemed to rise from the very depths of the ocean, booming its way to the surface, echoing across water and sand.

The cats and I froze, peering blindly towards the dark waves. And then it came again.

'*It's a monster,*' Philby whispered excitedly.

'*Oh really?*' Carrots quavered.

And then, in a flash, I knew what we were hearing.

'It's a WHALE!' I exclaimed in wonder and, springing up, I sped up the path shouting, 'DAVE . . . DAVE, come quickly!'

Behind me I heard Carrots puffing, '*What's a whale?*'

'*Shut up and run,*' hissed Philby.

We sat in the darkness for a long time listening to the whale calls. Eventually they became fainter, moving further out to sea. Finally they ceased altogether.

Ruth told us that whales came into the bay at certain times of the year to mate or calve. Very few people had ever heard them call. We were privileged, she said.

A few days later, the second significant event occurred. After undergoing a skin biopsy I was diagnosed with Systemic Lupus Erythematosus, an autoimmune disease in which the body is attacked by its own immune system.

God giveth and God taketh away.

To be honest, the diagnosis of Systemic Lupus did not come as a complete surprise. It was one of the many diseases I'd been tested for at Johannesburg General before the splenectomy. All the tests had proved negative, but the doctors had told me that the cortisone could be masking the results. When I was undergoing the tests, a friend of ours who was studying medicine had lent me a medical manual to peruse.

One evening he sat at my bedside in the hospital as I paged through the manual, seeking information on the various diseases.

'I hope it's not this one,' I said, pointing to a page.

'Which one?'

'Systemic Lupus.'

'Why?'

'Well, it states here that within five years of being diagnosed, there is a fatality rate of 90 per cent in Lupus patients.'

Looking horrified, he hastily removed the volume from my hands and left soon afterwards, taking the book with him.

Of course I should never have uttered those words, *I hope*

it's not this one. Fate has never needed much tempting. Something I wasn't aware of at the time was the fact that the book was very old, having been compiled many years before. When it was first published, only the very dire cases of Lupus were being diagnosed. As a result, the statistics were frightening.

Nevertheless, when Dr Smith leaned back in his chair, steepled his fingers and said, 'I think we can be fairly certain that you have Systemic Lupus,' I stared at him aghast, recalling the 90 per cent fatality rate. My immediate thought was, *Oh shit, Chrystal, now you're in big trouble. You're going to die*. I do not often swear and fortunately my sense of decorum prevented me from saying the words out loud. But on the way home, banging on the steering-wheel several times, I said, 'Oh shit, OH SHIT!'

Later that night I sat outside on the lawn while Dave bathed and fed Nic. Thick black clouds billowed across the sky obliterating the moon, and in my mind thoughts jostled for position in much the same way, obscuring the light. At my side, resting her body against mine, Whippy sat quietly, sensing my turmoil.

In the days that followed, I learned more about the disease. A friend of Dodo's, a retired medical doctor named Jean, came to see me. She brought me an exquisite orchid in a delicate glass vase and, even more exquisite, the news that Systemic Lupus could be effectively controlled.

Brendan and Mary gave me the telephone number of an acquaintance who had Lupus. A ballet dancer based in London, she was on holiday in Swaziland. We spoke on the telephone. She had been diagnosed several years before and was leading a perfectly normal life. Most of the time. When a crisis arose it was dealt with. As I replaced the receiver, the death sentence which had climbed up on to my shoulder in

Dr Smith's rooms quietly climbed off and walked out through the French windows. With a slight swagger.

I decided it was time to get fit. When my pregnancy had been confirmed in Swaziland I had stopped jogging. After Nic's birth my arthritis had become progressively worse and I had never resumed the daily run. Now it was time to start again.

With joyful abandon, Mandy, Whippy and Arrow entered into the spirit of getting fit. Thrilled by my new routine, every morning at dawn they would follow me happily down the path to the beach. Because of a sensitivity to sunlight, one of the symptoms of Lupus, I had to jog when the sun's rays were still weak. I didn't mind. As far as I was concerned, dawn was the best time of day. There was a sparkle to the world early in the morning. An iridescence of renewal. Sometimes even the dogs would sparkle as fine droplets of moisture formed on their fur.

One morning as we raced across the sand, I reflected on the role that they and the cats played in our lives. In a moment of deep insight, I knew that for me, and for Dave and Nic, much like the wind and rain and sunshine and the life-force itself, they were an underlying heartbeat.

As a rule, Dave preferred to run in the evenings, but sometimes he would join us in the morning. His pace was much faster than mine, his legs longer.

'Don't wait for me,' I'd call to him. 'I need to set my own pace.'

Unknowingly, those words spoken so casually were a finger on the pulse of Lupus.

Or, as Philby observed when consulted, *'Don't worry about it, just shut up and run.'*

And as we ran, our spirits thundered and crashed with the waves, then soared, swirling with the wind.

Epilogue

Dawn was breaking as we carried the crate down the path to the beach, puffing over the cool soft sand towards the waterline. Finally he murmured, 'OK, this is far enough,' and, turning, went back to help the others.

As I waited for them I gazed out over the sea. Like the day, it seemed barely awake, the water an opaque turquoise, grains of sand suspended in its silky depths. Waves curled lethargically, breaking with a faint *plop*. Hovering over them, a translucent mist caught the first weak rays of sunlight. Infinitely fine threads of vapour trapped the light, decking the ocean in a silver mantle of silence. The air was still, almost holding its breath in an expectant hush.

At last, when the four crates were lined up, he gave the signal and as we lifted the lids and tilted the crates, thirty-six penguins tumbled out on to the sand. Bewildered, they stood looking around them for a moment. Then their eyes focused on the sea and their bodies seemed to stiffen. Slowly, as if held in thrall, they moved towards the water. A few metres from its edge they began running, hurtling madly across the sand using both flippers and feet.

And then they were in the shallows and in the first wave and the second, diving, frolicking, their bodies sleek and clean.

Tears welled up in our eyes as we watched them move out into the bay. We stood in silence, eyes narrowed against the glare as they became mere black specks against the distant swells. When we could no longer see them at all, with a collective sigh we turned and walked slowly back up the beach towards the path.

As I stepped on to the first cobblestone, it occurred to me that there was a second path we were following now. A path lined with penguins.

Author's Note

Blossom, my nine-year-old blue-point Siamese, disappeared in Swaziland in November 1982. We advertised in *The Swazi Times* for one year after his disappearance, but there was no response.

Because this event was so sad, when I was writing this book I had to decide whether or not to include it. In the end I decided to do so because I have this faint hope that one day someone will contact me and say, 'You know that cat of yours, Blossom?'

And I'll say, 'Yes?'

And they'll say, 'Well, he spent the last ten years of his life with us.'

Blossom came from a Siamese breeder on the Bluff in Durban. When I went to select my kitten, there was this small slip of a thing, mostly ears, legs and tail, clinging to the wire roof of the cattery.

'Oh no, he's trying to escape again! It's the fourth time today,' the breeder huffed in exasperation.

'I'll have that one,' I said. So even then, the writing was on the wall.

Blossom loved people and roast chicken. Not necessarily in that order. At an early age, he developed an affinity for storm-water drains. Over the years I spent many hours stretched out flat on my stomach in the road, head inserted into the opening of one or another foul-smelling drain, calling, 'Blossom . . . Blossom,' in a syrupy voice.

One of his hobbies was catching spiders. Hulking great spiders, not little ones. Proudly, eyes squinting in excitement, he would present his victims to me, their long legs dangling from his mouth. Still twitching and jerking.

He feared nothing. Except nuns. This fear of nuns arose from the time he managed to get himself locked into the telephone booth of a nearby convent. He spent three days in that telephone booth. And he never made a sound. It was purely by chance that Sister Assumpta discovered his presence. Bending down to search for a pen she had dropped, as she groped under the low telephone table her hand encountered something furry.

'Oh dear God, it gave me quite a turn,' she told my mother.

Despite his disappearance, for many years afterwards I felt a sense of communication with Blossom. Then just after Nic turned ten, when he would've been nineteen, the communication ceased.

But the memories live on.